UNDER VINE
and FIG TREE

UNDER VINE
and FIG TREE

Biblical Theologies of Land
and the Palestinian-Israeli Conflict

Edited by
A l a i n E p p W e a v e r

Foreword by
J o h n A . L a p p

Cascadia

Publishing House
Telford, Pennsylvania

copublished with
Herald Press
Scottdale, Pennsylvania

Cascadia Publishing House LLC orders, information, reprint permissions:
contact@cascadiapublishinghouse.com
1-215-723-9125
126 Klingerman Road, Telford PA 18969
www.CascadiaPublishingHouse.com

Under Vine and Fig Tree
Copyright © 2007 by Cascadia Publishing House
a division of Cascadia Publishing House LLC, Telford, PA 18969
All rights reserved.
Copublished with Herald Press, Scottdale, PA
Library of Congress Catalog Number:2007018557
ISBN 13: 978-1-931038-45-4; **ISBN 10:** 1-931038-45-7
Book design by Cascadia Publishing House
Cover design by Gwen M. Stamm

The paper used in this publication is recycled and meets the
minimum requirements of American National Standard for Information Sciences—Permanence of Paper for Printed Library Materials,
ANSI Z39.48-1984.

All Bible quotations are used by permission, all rights reserved and,
unless otherwise noted, are from *The New Revised Standard Version of
the Bible*, copyright 1989, by the Division of Christian Education of the
National Council of the Churches of Christ in the USA.

Library of Congress Cataloguing-in-Publication Data
Under vine and fig tree : biblical theologies of land and the Pales-
tinian-Israeli conflict / edited by Alain Epp Weaver ; foreword by
John A. Lapp.
    p. cm.
Includes bibliographical references and indexes.
ISBN 978-1-931038-45-4 (6 x 9" trade pbk. : alk. paper)
 1. Land use--Biblical teaching. 2. Land tenure--Biblical teaching.
3. Arab-Israeli conflict. I. Weaver, Alain Epp. II. Title.

BS680.L25U53 2007
956.9405--dc22

2007018557

15 13 12 11 10 09 08 07   10 9 8 7 6 5 4 3 2 1

To Mennonite Central Committee's
Palestinian and Israeli partners

Contents

Foreword by John A. Lapp 9
Acknowledgments 11
Introduction: Under Vine and Fig Tree, by Alain Epp Weaver 13

Chapter 1: Independence or *Nakba*?
             A Sketch of the Palestinian-Israeli Conflict • 21
   Timothy Seidel
Chapter 2: Getting Grounded—The Land Belongs to God • 38
   Timothy Seidel
Chapter 3: Abraham's Promised Land • 49
   Dan Epp-Tiessen
Chapter 4: Conquering the Land • 62
   Esther Epp-Tiessen
Chapter 5: People Dispossessed of the Land • 75
   Esther Epp-Tiessen
Chapter 6: Living Justly in the Land • 86
   Christi Hoover Seidel
Chapter 7: Caring for the Land • 95
   Christi Hoover Seidel
Chapter 8: Security in the Land • 103
   Esther Epp-Tiessen
Chapter 9: The Land in the End Times: Part I • 117
   Dan Epp-Tiessen
Chapter 10: The Land in the End Times: Part II • 130
   Dan Epp-Tiessen

Chapter 11: Palestinian Christians: The Forgotten Faithful • 143
    Timothy Seidel
Chapter 12: Signs of the Kingdom in the Land • 153
    Christi Hoover Seidel

Timeline of the Palestinian-Israeli Conflict   162
Glossary of Terms   168
Resources for Further Study   180
Scripture Index   189
Subject Index   193
Maps   197
The Contributors   201

Foreword

A great gift God has given the contemporary church is the experience and insight of representatives who work in troublesome regions of the world. These ministry-inspired people acquire new languages, learn to appreciate diverse religious beliefs and practices, and strive to understand a variety of cultural patterns. Missioners who "take up residence" see human reality in new ways. They read the Scriptures with different lenses.

This inspiring yet disturbing volume demonstrates from one small part of the world how devout, international church representatives have been deeply moved by a situation of much pain and suffering.

The five authors of this volume provide a contemporary assessment of topics that international church workers have been experiencing and lamenting for more than sixty years. With candor, empathy for all parties, humility, and repentance, these authors demonstrate how the worldwide church might address such complex issues, particularly the control and use of land and water resources.

One of my early learnings about the dynamics of conflict in Israel-Palestine was that these tensions are a microcosm of conflicts all around the world. Each continent in the early twenty-first century has to deal with the realities of conquest and dispossession, of caring for the land and security in the land, of extraordinary wealth and power alongside abject poverty and powerlessness, of protracted war and millions of refugees, of ideologies and theologies which justify conquest and re-conquest, of allies who lend support to local partisans. Peoples on every continent hope to live under their own "vine and fig tree."

What gives a measure of uniqueness to the struggles in the Middle East is that the control of land has been repeatedly contested through the centuries. What is also unique is that the Jewish, Christian, and Muslim Scriptures address land issues so intensely. These three faiths also consider parts of, if not the entire region, to be endowed with special holiness. The shortage of water and the abundance of oil deepen the conflicts just at the moment military weaponry threatens the existence of humanity itself.

The special contribution of this volume is to connect the stories of suffering and struggle of families and villages with ancient and modern historic conflicts. The authors, reflecting their own Christian peace tradition, agonize over expectations for a just social order. They delve deeply into the Scriptures as a means of understanding conflict and for providing moral criteria for focusing on "the things that make for peace." Two chapters on "the land in the end times" provide especially helpful biblical interpretations for people confused by contemporary popular eschatology. The chapter on Palestinian Christians demonstrates how distressing such notions as rapture, return, and rule are for long-established Middle Eastern Christian communities.

The recurring references in these chapters to local partner organizations in Israel-Palestine highlights the significance of the dedication of this volume. There have always been local partners of international agencies and churches. In a post-colonial epoch it is especially important for agencies and churches to recognize that taking up residence requires deep identification and a cooperative style.

This is a carefully argued volume. Readers will find in these pages new energy for the urgent task of making peace. As Jesus on the mountain once said, this is "blessed work."

—*John A. Lapp*
  Executive Secretary Emeritus
  Mennonite Central Committee

Acknowledgments

*T*his book has been a collaborative effort from the beginning. Jan and Rick Janzen, Mennonite Central Committee (MCC) Area Directors for Europe and the Middle East, suggested this project as a follow-up to Sonia Weaver's book, *What is Palestine-Israel? Answers to Common Questions* (Herald Press, 2007). Sonia Weaver, who with her husband Alain spent most of the years from 1992-2006 working in the Middle East, did initial work brainstorming what such a study might address. Tim Seidel and the Applied Research Institute-Jerusalem (ARIJ), a long-time MCC partner in agricultural development and water recycling and harvesting, developed the maps included here. Ardell Stauffer compiled the indexes.

We are grateful to Calvin and Marie Shenk (formerly of Eastern Mennonite University and Mennonite Board of Missions), Harry Huebner (Canadian Mennonite University), and J. Daryl Byler (MCC Washington, D.C. office) for insightful comments on earlier drafts of this manuscript. All offered valuable suggestions. Any remaining errors or infelicities of style or theology are, of course, our responsibility, not theirs.

Finally, we wish to express our deep gratitude and humble appreciation for the ongoing witness of MCC's Palestinian and Israeli partner organizations, staffed by dynamic and faithful people committed to embodying the gospel and working for just and durable peace amid increasingly difficult circumstances. They never cease to inspire us, and it is to them that this book is dedicated.

Introduction:
Under Vine and Fig Tree

Alain Epp Weaver

*T*he prophet Micah's vision of a day when God's people will sit under vine and fig tree with no one to make them afraid (Mic. 4:4) provides the title for this book. The topic: how Christians should understand Palestine-Israel today in light of what Scripture has to say about right living in the land. Today neither Palestinians nor Israelis enjoy security. Both peoples yearn for peace, yet the conflict between them intensifies. As Christians, we often don't know what to think about this conflict. We are troubled by the ongoing violence and death we hear about through the mass media, but we don't know how to respond.

Our confusion about how to respond to the Palestinian-Israeli conflict tempts us to turn away in despair (or at times, if we are honest, in numb apathy). But we find that turning away isn't so easy. Christians, particularly in the United States, are deeply enmeshed in the ongoing Palestinian-Israeli conflict, whether we want to be or not. Each year the United States provides billions of dollars of assistance, directly and indirectly, to Israel, including massive military aid. American taxpayers, Christian and non-Christian, thus help support Israel's ongoing practices. At the same time, the cultural reach of Christian Zionist theology is wide, with organized Christian lobbies influencing national politics and with apocalyptic images of Armageddon and the rapture suffusing popular culture (witness the phenomenal publishing success of the *Left Behind* novels). Try as we might, we cannot escape the conflict.

Moreover, we know that there are good reasons why we should care about what happens in Palestine-Israel. The Palestinian-Israeli conflict creates unrest throughout the Middle East and beyond, a matter of global concern. Furthermore, as Christians we have compelling reasons to care. We should care about the fate and continuing witness of the church in Palestine-Israel, about the faithful but often forgotten Palestinian Christians who worship and glorify God in the Occupied Territories and inside Israel. As we Western Christians become aware and repent of anti-Jewish attitudes and practices in the church's history and today, we are driven to care about what Zionism and the state of Israel will mean for the future of Jewish life and witness. And as a people who await the coming of new heavens and a new earth, we should pray for the land in which God's victory over the powers of sin and death was assured to give humanity a foretaste of God's kingdom of justice, peace, and reconciliation.

This book seeks to focus our minds and our hearts on the contemporary realities of violence and dispossession in Palestine-Israel by grounding us in Scripture. We seek to read biblical texts about land alongside stories from Palestinians and Israelis, trusting that God's Word holds good news for both peoples. Throughout the following chapters, we struggle with questions that often arise regarding the Bible and the Palestinian-Israeli conflict. What does the Bible tell us about land that might illuminate the ongoing conflict between the two peoples? How do God's promises of land to Abraham and his descendants connect to contemporary claims over the land? What is the relationship between today's events in Israel and the end times? What are ways Scripture is used to justify dispossession and unjust practices in the land? What are ways we can receive as God's Word portions of Scripture, such as the conquest narratives of Joshua and Judges, which trouble us with their apparent divine justification of ethnic cleansing? What positive visions of justice and reconciliation in the land does the Bible offer us?

For nearly six decades Mennonites have lived and worked alongside Palestinians and Israelis, hearing from friends, neighbors, and colleagues about their stories of violence and dispossession and their hopes for futures of secure dwellings. It was the massive dispossession of Palestinian refugees in 1948 that first brought Mennonite Central Committee (MCC) to the region. Mennonites have also, however, heard from Israeli Jews about the Jewish history of violence at the hands of Western Christians and about how many Jews, Israelis and non-Israelis, view the state of Israel as a safe haven from anti-Jewish persecution.

While Zionism pre-dates the Holocaust by several decades, one cannot, as the late Palestinian writer Edward Said underscored, understand the visceral attachment of many Jews to the state of Israel without the context of the Holocaust. Many Holocaust survivors ended up in Israel (in large part because many Western countries, including the United States, admitted limited numbers of Jewish refugees). The Holocaust does not, of course, justify or excuse particular actions of the state of Israel, but it must be acknowledged if one is to understand Israeli fears and Jewish attachment to the state of Israel. Many Jews, meanwhile, find it tragic that the Jewish people, subject for centuries to mistreatment, violence, and most recently genocide by their supposedly Christian neighbors, now carry out policies that dispossess another people. Both Israelis and Palestinians are marked by histories of violence and dispossession, and yearn for security under vine and fig tree.

Over the past decades, Mennonites in the Middle East have also learned from Muslim friends and colleagues about the hostilities and suspicions created by Western crusades and more recently by various forms of colonialist domination. Finding creative ways to repent of Western Christianity's checkered past toward Muslims (and toward Middle Eastern Christians) is a vitally important task. Reflections on Mennonite experience in various global contexts of forging bonds of friendship across Muslims-Christian divides can be found in a forthcoming(2007) Cascadia book I have edited with Peter Dula, *Borders and Bridges: Mennonite Witness in a Religiously Diverse World*.

This book grows out of MCC's decades of work alongside Palestinians (and more recently Israelis). MCC was one of the first international organizations to respond to the Palestinian refugee crisis of 1948—what Palestinians refer to as the *Nakba*, Arabic for catastrophe. Mennonite volunteers distributed relief

supplies to the tens of thousands of Palestinian refugees who
had congregated in the refugee camps around Jericho. Later
MCC established Christian schools in Hebron and Beit Jala and
organized self-help projects for Palestinian women.

During the 1970s, following the Israeli occupation of the
West Bank, MCC worked with Palestinian farmers, introducing
drip irrigation and distributing seedlings as ways of helping
Palestinian farmers protect their land from Israeli confiscation.
From the 1980s onward, MCC has worked in partnership with
Palestinian and, more recently, Israeli initiatives. Today MCC's
work focuses on maximizing Palestinian access to water resources, supporting the ministries of the Palestinian church and
encouraging Israeli and Palestinian peacebuilding initiatives.

Mennonites in Palestine-Israel, along with workers serving
other international Christian organizations, such as World Vision, Lutheran World Federation, and Catholic Relief Services,
are routinely asked about how the Bible relates to the continuing
conflict between Palestinians and Israelis. Some who ask this
question believe that criticism of the state of Israel is wrong; they
are convinced that Israel is playing a key role in the events leading up to the end of time and Jesus' second coming. Others ask
because they are struggling with the Bible's different theologies
of land, including, for example, parts of Scripture that disturb
many Christians, such as the depictions of the violent conquest
of the land of Canaan.

Given the frequency of such questions, MCC decided that it
would be valuable to put together a short study about biblical
theologies of land and their relationship to the Palestinian-Israeli conflict. In autumn 2005, the MCC Palestine peace workers,
Timothy Seidel and Christi Hoover Seidel, were joined for three
months by Esther Epp-Tiessen, MCC Canada peace and justice
coordinator, and Dan Epp-Tiessen, professor of Old Testament at
Canadian Mennonite University. Listening closely to the voices
of MCC's Israeli and Palestinian partners, particularly the voices
of Palestinian Christians, these writers, with input from MCC
workers Sonia and Alain Epp Weaver, compiled the reflections
that follow.

After an initial chapter sketching the history of the Palestinian-Israeli conflict, the authors proceed to tackle such matters as
biblical perspectives on land ownership; the character of biblical

promises of land; experiences of dispossession viewed from a scriptural angle; and ways to understand end-times, or apocalyptic, material in relationship to contemporary events. Most chapters include discussion questions and suggestions for action; resources for further reading, learning, and action are included at the end of the book, along with a glossary of frequently used terms.

We have sought in this book to give voice to our conviction that the Bible speaks a word of hope to Palestinians and Israelis, a hope that a shared future in the land is possible in which both peoples might live securely under vine and fig tree. This is our answer to the questions we receive from concerned Christians about how the Bible and the Palestinian-Israeli conflict relate. We recognize that for Christians for whom the state of Israel is the fulfillment of biblical prophecy and a sign of the imminent end of the world, our readings of Scripture and our understanding of the Palestinian-Israeli conflict may be jarring, perhaps even offensive. Christians disagree about a wide variety of matters, and the Palestinian-Israeli conflict is one that generates heated passions. We pray that this book might be a way to begin, rather than end, a conversation about a hotly contested issue among Christians.

Palestinians and Israelis with whom we have worked have often stressed that the Palestinian-Israeli conflict is at root a political, not a religious, conflict. This claim captures the important insight that the Palestinian-Israeli conflict should be understood in comparison with other global instances of colonialism. That said, many Palestinian Christians, Palestinian Muslims, and Israeli Jews do give a religious interpretation to the conflict. In conversation with Palestinian Christians, we have sought here to offer theological reflections on land grounded in the Christian story which celebrate the gift of land as a place where all of God's children might live together in equality and security. Having been privileged to work together with deeply committed Palestinian Muslims, and Israeli Jews, we know that similar positive visions of land could also be offered by Jews and Muslims.

Some comments on names are in order. Names of countries and territories in the Middle East can be matters of fierce contention. Following international usage, we use Occupied Territories to refer to the West Bank, East Jerusalem, and the Gaza Strip, all territories militarily occupied by Israel since June 1967. Palestine-Israel refers to the strip of land from the Jordan River in the east to the Mediterranean Sea in the west, from the Upper Galilee in the north down to the southern Negev (Hebrew)/Naqab (Arabic) desert in the south. Part of the Ottoman Empire before World War I, this strip of land was called Palestine during the years of the British Mandate (from the 1920s until 1948). Following the war of 1948, the land of Palestine became home to the new state of Israel (in seventy-eight percent of historical Palestine), with the remaining territory occupied by Jordan (the West Bank and East Jerusalem) and Egypt (the Gaza Strip).

Today, when some people say "Palestine," they refer to the state that may or may not emerge in some form in all or parts of the Occupied Territories. In this book we speak of Palestine-Israel to recognize that the historical land of Palestine is today home to two nations. These two national groups live in conditions of marked inequality. In the future visions of reconciliation, they may live together, side-by-side, in two separate viable states, or they may live together in one binational state as equal citizens before the law. Using the name *Palestine-Israel* signals our hope that such reconciliation will one day materialize.

As Christians from the United States and Canada, the authors of this volume recognize that we can make no claim to special knowledge about what makes for right living in the land. Our communities and our nations have often failed, quite dramatically, to practice justice in the land and have turned away from stories of dispossession, especially of indigenous First Nations/Native North American peoples among us. We are acutely aware that Mennonite congregations in Canada and the United States are no freer of the sin of anti-Judaism than other Christian bodies, and we are also mindful that Mennonites in North America, like other Christians, have too often failed to remember (or even be aware of) the existence and witness of the Palestinian churches.

It is in a spirit of humility and repentance, then, in awareness that we have much to learn about right living in the land, that we offer this study to the wider church. Our prayer is that Palestinians and Israelis might soon experience in reality Micah's vision of all persons sitting securely under vine and fig tree.

UNDER VINE
and FIG TREE

Chapter 1

Independence or *Nakba*? A Sketch of the Palestinian-Israeli Conflict

Timothy Seidel

*H*ow we look at history strongly influences what that past says to us about who we are, where we are, where we come from, and where we are going. For one's perspective, one's frame of reference, is like a prism. It refracts the light of time in a given manner to illuminate (or obscure) a particular set of historical events. For example, what is "good news" in the grand telling of events for victors in battle can often sound like bad news to those seeing history "from below."

We have much to learn from the perspective of the underside of history. To strive for justice, peace, and reconciliation means to be challenged to recognize whom we exclude in our telling of history, whose voices we leave out. Telling the story of Zionism and the foundation of the state of Israel is no exception to this truism. One's frame of reference shapes how one perceives the events of 1948 that led to Israel's formation. Our task in this book of examining how the Palestinian-Israeli conflict can be understood in light of biblical theologies of land requires that we first look at the differing perspectives on that conflict's history.

For example, for most Israeli Jews, May 14, 1948, is Independence Day—a heroic story of freedom, liberty, and success in overcoming great difficulties. No longer would Jews live the uncertain life of minority communities; rather, they would be masters of their own fate in their own land. But for Palestinians, May 15, 1948, is known as the *Nakba*, an Arabic word meaning "catastrophe." Nakba refers to the massive dispossession of the majority of the Palestinian people during the period of 1947 to 1949. Between 750,000 to 900,000 Palestinians became refugees, either having been expelled by the Zionist militias like the Palmach or having fled for their lives during the fighting. Meanwhile, Israeli military forces destroyed over 500 Palestinian villages. Even Palestinians who remained inside what became Israel experienced dispossession, with tens of thousands of Palestinians becoming internally displaced persons, alienated from their land.

Scores of book-length manuscripts have been written about the history of the Palestinian-Israeli conflict. Any concise telling of this story must necessarily be selective. This all-too-brief historical sketch will examine why a history identified by many Israelis as a history of independence and liberation has for Palestinians been a history of dispossession and catastrophe.

This survey begins at the end of the nineteenth century.[1] This is not to say that the history preceding these years is unimportant but simply to stress the modern nature of the current conflict. Spending too much time in premodern history unhelpfully reinforces the popular notion that the conflict between Palestinians and Israelis is an "age-old" conflict, and therefore intractable. Instead, we should view the Palestinian-Israeli conflict as a modern phenomenon, one that began around the turn of the twentieth century.

Furthermore, while religious symbols and vocabulary have often contributed to the rhetoric of the conflict, religion is arguably not the cause of the conflict. Rather, the conflict has essentially been a struggle over land, a struggle between a settler-colonialist movement (Zionism) looking for liberation, for a land without a people for a people without a land—and the anti-colonialist resistance of the people already living on land that turned out not to be empty after all.[2] What was independence for one was catastrophe for the other.

"INDEPENDENCE"

Independence Day in Israel is a time of celebration and remembrance. In May every year the sure signs of celebration are ubiquitous: flags hanging from windows and fluttering from car antennas, families and friends gathering in parks for picnics and barbecues, and fireworks exploding in the evening sky. On Independence Day, Israelis remember their history, a history they narrate as a movement from the uncertainty of life as an often-oppressed minority to liberation. Independence Day is thus the key celebration of Zionism—the modern nationalist movement that gave birth to the state of Israel.

Zionism emerged as a European movement in the nineteenth century seeking to solve the problem of anti-Judaism that European Jewish communities had faced for centuries. Early Zionist leaders like the Austrian Theodor Herzl advocated the creation of a Jewish state, reasoning that just like the French had France and the Germans had Germany, so Jews should have their own state. While early Zionists considered Uganda and Argentina as possible locations for this proposed state, most assumed Palestine would be the natural location. In the late nineteenth century, the land of Palestine was part of the Ottoman Empire, which for 400 years had ruled over most of the Middle East. Around half a million people lived in Palestine. Most were Muslim, while about 60,000 were Christian and 20,000 were Jews. All spoke Arabic.[3]

For Herzl, Zionism meant the reinvention of Judaism not as a religion but as the ideology of a nation.[4] For most religious Jews of the time, Zionism bordered on blasphemy, a human attempt to intervene on God's behalf to do the Messiah's job of bringing them out of exile. While religious variations of Zionism later developed, initially Zionism had an aggressively secular character. While Zionism was initially a minority phenomenon within European Jewry, that did not stop the determined minority. The early 1880s saw the first wave of Jewish immigration (what the Zionists termed *aliyah,* or ascent, to Palestine). Second and third waves followed over the ensuing decades.

After World War I, the League of Nations divided the Arab lands of the defeated and dissolved Ottoman Empire into territories called mandates. These mandates were eventually to become nation-states for the indigenous people. Britain accepted the mandate for Palestine in 1922, and with it the responsibility to turn the country over to self-rule.

Britain, however, had made a conflicting pledge in the form of the Balfour Declaration of 1917—a letter sent by British Foreign Secretary Arthur James Balfour to Zionist leader Baron de Rothschild promising British support for the establishment of a Jewish national home in Palestine. Although the Zionist leadership at times felt that the British Mandate authorities placed too many restrictions on Jewish immigration to Palestine, Britain's Balfour commitments inexorably reshaped the demographic balance on the land, a fact not missed by the Palestinian Arab population. Throughout the years of the British Mandate, tensions routinely flared, sometimes violently, between Palestinians and Zionist settlers and between both communities and the British authorities.

Despite Britain's Balfour commitments, Jewish immigration to Palestine remained relatively limited during the Mandate period. It was in the wake of the Holocaust, or *Shoah*, in which the Nazi regime systematically murdered six million Jews, that Jewish immigration surged. By 1946, around 680,000 Jews were living in Palestine. The horrific experience of the Shoah provided for many Jews grim confirmation of the Zionist claim that minority life in the diaspora was inherently unstable and untenable and gave credibility to the Zionist program of setting up a Jewish state that would be a safe haven from anti-Judaism. Zionism, to be sure, did not begin with the Holocaust. One cannot, however, understand the visceral attachment of many Jews to the state of Israel apart from the trauma of the Holocaust. The state of Israel, for many Jews, appeared as a beacon of hope, promising safety from persecution and subjugation.

The conflict between Jews and Arabs in Palestine, in the Zionist telling of this story, came to a head following the British decision to relinquish its mandate to the League of Nation's successor, the United Nations (UN), and the passage of UN General Assembly Resolution 181, also known as the "partition plan." The partition plan called for Palestine to be divided into a Jewish state (ca. fifty-six percent of Palestine) and an Arab state (ca. forty-three percent of the land), with Jerusalem as an international protectorate.

The mainstream Zionist leaders accepted the UN plan even though it did not account for all of Zionism's territorial ambitions. The Palestinians, the neighboring Arab states, and the Arab League rejected it. The ensuing struggle, according to traditional Israeli accounts, was an unequal contest between a Jewish David and an Arab Goliath. Great Britain did everything in its power toward the end of the Palestine Mandate to frustrate the establishment of the Jewish state, according to standard Israeli histories. Then, when Britain ended its Mandate and the state of Israel was declared on May 14, 1948, five Arab states sent their armies into Palestine with the firm intention of strangling the Jewish state at birth. The infant Jewish state, on this telling, fought a desperate, heroic, and ultimately successful battle for survival against overwhelming odds.

When the armistice lines were drawn in 1949, Israel had gained control of seventy-eight percent of British Mandatory Palestine, including some of the land designated by the United Nations for a Palestinian Arab state, while East Jerusalem and the West Bank of the Jordan River were occupied by Jordan, with the Gaza Strip occupied by Egypt. After the war, in this telling of the story, Israeli leaders sought peace with all their heart and might but there was no one to talk to on the other side. Arab intransigence alone, it was believed, was responsible for the political deadlock and for what ultimately led to the Six-Day War. In that June 1967 war Israel attacked Egypt, claiming it was acting preemptively, and occupied East Jerusalem, the West Bank, the Gaza Strip, the Egyptian Sinai, and the Syrian Golan Heights.

After expanding the Jerusalem municipal boundaries, Israel extended its laws over East Jerusalem and placed the rest of the occupied Palestinian territories under military rule. Israel would later withdraw from the Sinai as part of the Camp David accords of the late 1970s and the early 1980s and sign peace treaties with Egypt and Jordan. However, the sense that there is no "partner for peace" continues to shape Israeli consciousness. Palestinian resistance is viewed as terrorism that seeks to obliterate Israel's existence. Each suicide bombing in Tel Aviv and Jerusalem reinforces Israel's sense of being embattled.

Zionism promised a safe haven for Jews, an independent state in which the Jewish people would be free of the worries of hostile neighbors and the uncertainties of minority life. Many Israelis today still cling to this dream of national independence as a guarantor of security, even as daily Israeli existence is marked by feelings of insecurity. Not all Israelis, however, accept the story of Zionism and Israel's foundation as a simple story of liberation and independence; some Israelis committed to reconciliation believe that durable peace must be built on a deeper understanding of what Israel's "independence" has meant for their Palestinian neighbors.

"NAKBA"

For several years now, Israelis and Palestinians have been meeting together to remember another side of this story. Through meetings organized by the Israeli Zochrot Association, Israeli Jews and internally displaced Palestinians return to the sites of Palestinian villages destroyed in 1948 (in some cases to the very parks built on the ruins of these villages, parks to which many Israelis go to celebrate Independence Day) to tell another story. That alternate narrative is one of dispossession for Palestinians that has continued unabated to this day. These groups of Israelis and Palestinians post signs marking the ruined buildings as mosques, churches, or private residences, or erect street signs with original Arabic street names, believing that remembering the past is an indispensable component of moving toward a future of peaceful coexistence.

For Palestinians, the twentieth century has been a story of Palestinian subjugation by colonial powers. Great Britain and France carved up the Middle East between them in the Sykes-Picot agreements of 1916 as World War I came to a close, even as Britain promised independence to Arab leaders in exchange for help in battling the Ottomans during the war, promises that conflicted with British commitments to the Zionist leadership in the 1917 Balfour Declaration. Britain accepted the League of Nations' mandate for Palestine in 1922 without consent of the Palestinians—indeed, in opposition to the Palestinians' expressed desires for independence. Palestinians, meanwhile, were suspicious of Britain's pledge of support for the establishment of a

Jewish national home, which, as historian Rashid Khalidi observes, "they rightly feared would inexorably develop into an exclusively Jewish state in their homeland and at their expense."[5]

Palestinians regarded the subsequent United Nations partition plan of 1947 as another chapter in this story of disenfranchisement. Palestinians rejected the partition plan as unfair, noting that under the plan over half of Palestine, including the most fertile land, would go to a Jewish state at a time the Jewish community composed a third of the total population and owned only six percent of the land.

Palestinian-Israeli tensions reached a head after the partition plan was announced. By 1948, war in Palestine was underway. Britain had ended its mandate in May 1948, and Israel had declared independence on May 14. By the time the British had left, fully one third of the Palestinian population had already been expelled from their homes. In April 1948, for example, Zionist forces massacred over one hundred Palestinians in Deir Yassin, a village west of Jerusalem. David Ben-Gurion, who became Israel's first prime minister, ordered Zionist forces to conquer Arab districts around Jerusalem and resettle them with Jews.

The end of the British mandate actually signaled the end of the first phase of the 1948 war, which had lasted from December 1947 to May 1948. The beginning of a second phase saw Arab armies appearing for the first time. Despite the images of a Jewish David against an Arab Goliath throughout the war, Zionist forces outnumbered all Arab forces. Furthermore, during the first truce Israel violated the UN embargo and imported arms from the Eastern bloc while the Arab armies failed to replenish their arms supplies, due to Britain's resolve to observe the UN arms embargo on the warring parties. Illicit arms imports decisively tipped the military balance in favor of Israel. The Zionist forces not only outnumbered but also outgunned their opponents. The final outcome of the war was not a miracle but a reflection of the underlying Arab-Israeli military balance.[6]

By the end of the fighting, between 750,000 and 900,000 Palestinians had become refugees, having been forcefully expelled or having fled under the threat of expulsion. Thousands died in massacres. Over 500 Palestinian villages and towns were depopulated and destroyed. This represented two-thirds of the entire Palestinian people.

Roughly 150,000 Palestinians stayed in what became the state of Israel. Many became "internally displaced persons"—refugees expelled from their homes but who became citizens of the state of Israel. For Palestinians, the experience of 1948 devastated the entire society. It was, in short, a catastrophe, a Nakba. "We now have a term to describe what Israel did to the Palestinians in 1948 which did not exist then," Israeli historian Avi Shlaim poignantly observes—"ethnic cleansing."[7]

The United Nations, in General Assembly Resolution 194, declared that Palestinian refugees ready to live at peace with their neighbors should be allowed to return to their homes and properties at the earliest possible date. Nearly six decades later, Israel maintains its adamant refusal to allow refugees to return home.

In late 1948, Israel instituted an anti-repatriation policy, which included, according to Israeli historian Ilan Pappé, "either the total destruction or full Jewish take-over of every Palestinian house and dwelling, both of the villages and the urban neighborhoods,"[8] with the hasty erection of Jewish settlements on top of the hundreds of Palestinian villages destroyed in 1948. Palestinian refugee property, meanwhile, was confiscated by Israel under its Absentee Property Law. Thousands of Palestinians who had remained inside Israel also lost their land under this law. Through the law Israel classified them as "present absentees." Meanwhile, Israel's Law of Return, which entitled any Jew to full Israeli citizenship, helped large-scale Jewish immigration to Israel from Europe, North Africa, and Asia.

Israel commenced a process of judaizing the new state in the coastal plain between Tel Aviv and Haifa, in the Negev, and in the Galilee, areas from which Palestinians had been driven. "A naming committee granted the new settlements Hebraized versions of the original Arab names," notes Pappé.[9] Ben-Gurion, meanwhile, "personally supervised a large project to give 'Hebrew names to all the places, mountains, valleys, springs, and roads, etc.' in the country. This act of 'memoricide' was completed in 1951."[10] While the Palestinian-Arab markers on the landscape were buried, Palestinian citizens inside Israel lived under strict military law during the 1950s and into the 1960s.

The Six Day War of 1967 also saw the continuation of the Palestinian story of dispossession. Another 400,000 Palestinians were driven from their homes during the war. Half of them, already refugees from 1948, were now refugees twice over. Israel extended its laws over East Jerusalem and placed the rest of the West Bank (along with the Gaza Strip) under military rule, denying the population living in these territories basic human or civic rights.[11] Palestinian resistance to the occupation—both violent and nonviolent—was met with overwhelming force by the Israeli military, including various forms of collective punishment such as house demolitions, expulsions, and arrests without trial.

The UN responded to the Six Day War by passing Security Council Resolution 242, which called for the withdrawal of Israeli troops from the newly occupied territories. UNSC 242 (and later UNSC 338) became the internationally accepted guideline for a just and lasting peace in the Middle East. The resolutions served as the basis for subsequent peace agreements between Israel, on the one hand, and Jordan and Egypt, on the other. Citing these peace agreements, which involved the full Israeli withdrawal from occupied Egyptian and Jordanian territory in exchange for peace, Palestinians insist that durable peace with Israel must mean full Israeli withdrawal from East Jerusalem, the West Bank, and the Gaza Strip.

Israel did not comply with UNSC 242 but instead began to build illegal settlements on the newly occupied land in violation of the Fourth Geneva Convention, which prohibits occupying powers from moving their civilian population into occupied territories. Slowly but surely over the ensuing decades the geography of the Occupied Territories began to change, with Jewish-only settlements breaking up territorial connections among Palestinian population centers and dominating the landscape.

Starting in the mid-1960s, Palestinian resistance coalesced around the Palestine Liberation Organization (PLO), which in 1974 was recognized by the Arab League as the sole legitimate representative of the Palestinian people, both inside Palestine and in the diaspora. In December 1987, the Palestinian uprising or *intifada* (Arabic for "shaking off") began in the Occupied Territories. After decades of occupation, economic exploitation, and human rights violations, the Palestinian people began a collective uprising against the Israeli occupation in the West Bank and Gaza Strip. Demonstrations, rock throwing, strikes, boy-cotts of Israeli goods, tax resistance, and general unrest lasted for six years. Regrettably, resistance to the occupation sometimes turned violent, with attacks on soldiers and civilians. The Israeli military responded with harsh measures, such as travel restric-tions and military curfews, school and university closures, and mass arrests.

In November 1988, meanwhile, the PLO issued its "Declara-tion of Independence," which highlighted the PLO's readiness to make peace on the basis of UNSC 242 and 338. In 1993, after six years of intifada, Israel and the PLO began secret talks that led to the signing of a series of agreements known collectively as the Oslo Accords. The accords set up the Palestinian Authority (PA) as a semi-autonomous body in 1994 in parts of the Occupied Ter-ritories.

The West Bank, for example, was divided into three areas of control. After several years of negotiated withdrawals, the West Bank in the year 2000 consisted of three different types of juris-diction: Area A (seventeen percent), comprising Palestinian cities, came under direct Palestinian control; in Area B (twenty-four percent), Palestinians had control over civilian affairs while Israel kept security responsibilities; and in Area C (fifty-nine percent) Israel maintained full authority. In the heady days of 1992 to 1994, many Palestinians anticipated that further negotia-tions would lead to a full withdrawal from all of the Occupied Territories, setting the stage for a lasting peace agreement.

But by 1997, the peace process had frozen and it became clear that the Oslo process had become a way to solidify Israel's control over the Occupied Territories. "It was the imbalance of power," explains Israeli historian Pappé, "tilting dramatically in Israel's favour, which determined how the principles would be translated into reality."[12] Oslo had deferred the conflict's core is-sues—the fate of Jerusalem, settlements, and refugees, along with the question of final borders and control of water re-sources—to "final status" negotiations.

The imbalance of power, however, meant that Israel could postpone final status negotiations indefinitely while creating facts on the ground that would make its control over the Occu-pied Territories permanent. During the late 1990s, Palestinians faced new restrictions on movement, an increase in the number of checkpoints, isolation from Jerusalem, and extensive land confiscations for new and expanded Israeli settlements. Far from an end to the occupation, Israeli control in fact intensified. Israel doubled its settlement activity in the occupied West Bank (including East Jerusalem) in the seven years following the Oslo agreements. Settlers in the Occupied Territories in 1993 numbered 220,000; by 2000 the number had grown to 450,000.

Even as peace talks foundered, the much-hoped-for U.S.-sponsored Camp David summit between Palestinians and Israelis convened in summer 2000. During the talks, Israel proposed to withdraw from much of the Occupied Territories, but the exact nature of what was proposed is hotly contested among the participants. Palestinians claim that the Israeli proposal denied Palestinians control over borders, airspace, and water resources, while legitimizing and expanding many Israeli settlement blocs. For Palestinians, the Oslo process had meant giving up seventy-eight percent of historical Palestine upfront, with an eye to establishing a state made up of the remaining twenty-two percent. Israel, for its part, saw the remaining twenty-two percent as up for negotiation. This summit ended predictably without reaching an agreement. Israelis claimed that Palestinians had turned down a "generous offer," while Palestinians argued that this offer meant Palestinians accepting a dismembered homeland.

Shortly after the failed Camp David summit, the second intifada broke out, initially following a provocative visit by Ariel Sharon, then leader of the opposition Likud party, to the Haram al-Sharif (the Noble Sanctuary), the third holiest site in Islam and also located on the Temple Mount. Popular demonstrations sprang up throughout the Occupied Territories and among Palestinians inside Israel, demonstrations met by brute force. Violence escalated on both sides over the ensuing weeks and months, the death and injury tolls rose, and the remnants of the peace process broke down. While some Palestinians called for nonviolent forms of resistance, militant groups carried out a variety of violent attacks both in the Occupied Territories and inside Israel, including suicide bombings in the heart of Israeli cities. Some Israelis, meanwhile, appealed for renewed peace efforts built on the foundation of justice, even as the Israeli military intensified its actions against Palestinians.

In spring 2002, Israel, under then-Prime Minister Ariel Sharon, re-invaded nearly all Palestinian areas evacuated during the Oslo process as part of its "Operation Defensive Shield." In this invasion, Israel laid siege to the Church of the Nativity in Bethlehem, entered Ramallah, leveled the heart of the Jenin refugee camp, destroyed the Old City of Nablus, and imposed week-and-even-months-long curfews on civilian populations. The Palestinian Authority was reduced from a state-in-the-making to little more than a largely disconnected network of village and town councils.

Citing the need for greater security, Israel also began in 2002 construction on what it called a "security fence" inside the West Bank. A network of concrete walls up to nine meters (about thirty feet) in height and electronically monitored areas, fences, patrol roads, and barbed wire, this separation barrier became part of a wider Israeli strategy known variously as "disengagement," "unilateral separation," or "convergence." Sharon presented his disengagement plan in 2004, a unilateral Israeli initiative to withdraw its military presence from most of the Gaza Strip (save the border areas) and select parts of the northern West Bank.

In August 2005, Israel executed its unilateral disengagement from Gaza by removing all Gaza settlers as well as dismantling four small, isolated settlements in the northern West Bank. The dismantled settlements accounted for two percent of the total settler population, while at the same time the overall settler population in the West Bank had increased by four percent during the years of Sharon's rule. Israeli officials explained to the Israeli public that the disengagement process helped freeze the peace process and the idea of a Palestinian state.

In 2006, Israel declared its intention to continue its unilateral actions in a "convergence" plan that would formally annex major settlement blocs in the West Bank as well as the Jordan Valley in an attempt to set the final borders of the state of Israel unilaterally. Palestinian population centers became increasingly circumscribed by walls and fences, and the Palestinian economy deteriorated. The election of the Islamist Hamas party (not a member of the PLO) to the Palestinian Legislative Council and to the ministries of the Palestinian Authority in January 2006 reflected Palestinian frustration with the PLO's inability to establish a viable state in all of the Occupied Territories. Hamas' victory, meanwhile, confirmed for Israel that it had no partner.

Following the election of Hamas, much of the international community, led by the United States, imposed a boycott on the Palestinian Authority, demanding that Hamas recognize Israel and commit itself to existing peace agreements between Israel and the PLO. Hamas, for its part, said that it was ready to offer Israel a long-term truce. For ordinary Palestinians, this boycott had devastating economic and social effects. Unemployment soared throughout the Occupied Territories; poverty levels went up to eighty percent in the Gaza Strip, as this densely populated piece of land was increasingly cut off from the outside world into what one Israeli human rights organization called "one big prison."

It was in this context that in the summer of 2006 one Israeli soldier was abducted by Palestinian groups in Gaza and two more by the Lebanese group Hezbollah in northern Israel. In response, Israel launched major military campaigns against Lebanon and Gaza. These campaigns saw the deaths of over 1,000 Lebanese, 300 Palestinians, and 100 Israelis. Hundreds of thousands of Lebanese and many Gazans were displaced from their homes. Israel was widely condemned for its disproportionate actions against the people of Lebanon and Gaza. Unexploded ordnance from Israeli cluster bombs littered the countryside of southern Lebanon, and Gaza's infrastructure was decimated.

The Israeli siege on Gaza continued long after bombardment had ended. These economic pressures fostered internal Palestinian tension, especially in Gaza, between Fatah and Hamas, tension that came to a head in early 2007, with heavy Palestinian internal fighting. A Palestinian Authority national unity government was eventually formed, including Fatah, Hamas, and other major political factions, calming these internal tensions. However, this unity government was not accepted by Israel and was received coldly by the United States and much of the international community, which maintained its demand that Hamas must first officially recognize Israel in order for economic sanctions to be lifted.

DISPOSSESSION CONTINUED

Despite the optimism that accompanied reports on the Israeli disengagement from Gaza, the expansion of Israeli domination over Palestinian life and land and the story of Palestinian dispossession have continued. Whether it was through more land being expropriated for the construction of the 430-mile (680 km) separation barrier cutting through the West Bank, the dramatic growth of illegal settlements, including around Jerusalem, or the proliferation of checkpoints and roadblocks that obstructed mobility, Palestinian livelihoods continued to be devastated by military occupation. The experience of dispossession proceeded unabated.

Unfortunately, it appears this separation barrier—though condemned as illegal in 2004 by the International Court of Justice—will become Israel's new border, leaving a Palestinian quasi-state composed of several isolated islands of land on roughly forty to fifty percent of the West Bank. Palestinians will be confined to what they call "reservations," or, evoking South Africa under apartheid, "Bantustans," which will be partly connected by a network of tunnels controlled by Israel. Industrial zones may then be established at the edges of these areas so that businesses can take advantage of a cheap, imprisoned labor pool. Pappé describes the goal of this Israeli unilateralism thusly: "a strong Jewish state dominating a small Palestinian protectorate, without a solution to the refugee problem or a significant Palestinian presence or sovereignty in Jerusalem."[13]

Today researchers estimate that over seven million Palestinians—about three-quarters of the total Palestinian population (and about one-third of the global refugee population)—live as refugees and internally displaced persons in the Occupied Territories and Israel as well as in other countries like Jordan, Syria, and Lebanon. Many still hold the land deeds to the properties they were expelled from and the keys to the homes from which they were driven. They wait for their opportunity to choose whether or not to return. Even as their dispossession continues to be unaddressed, so do new forms of dispossession mark Palestinian life in the Occupied Territories.

The Nakba is the story of all the people of Palestine-Israel. Though the dominant narrative of Zionism is one of "liberation" for Israeli Jews, it is a false liberation; Palestinian dispossession is its price. True liberation for Israelis and Palestinians alike, one could suggest, means confronting this history of dispossession so that new futures of coexistence and reconciliation might be imagined. Israeli historian Avi Shlaim explains that

> The evidence that we have at our disposal today, makes it patently clear, and indeed beyond dispute, that the creation of the state of Israel involved a monumental injustice to the Palestinians. Unless and until Israel acknowledges its share of the moral responsibility for the creation of the Palestinian refugee problem, this dispute will not be solved.[14]

The late Palestinian scholar Edward Said concurred with Shlaim, noting that

> if Israelis and Palestinians are to learn to coexist peacefully side by side, it is essential that they understand their own history and each other's history. It is not enough for each side to examine critically its own actions in 1948. We must have a common and comprehensive picture of what happened in the war to deal with its consequences, to find a solution to this tragic conflict.[15]

Only in naming the past are we brought to a place where we might bring change and foster hope for the future. Liberation is something so many of the oppressed in this world seek. But for a lasting and secure peace born of justice, true liberation must be life-giving for all in the land. In Palestine-Israel, what if true liberation in this sense, for both Israelis and Palestinians, means the sharing of land on the basis of equality for all?

QUESTIONS FOR DISCUSSION

1. The land of most of the more than 500 villages destroyed in 1948 does not house Israeli communities. What prevents Palestinian refugees from returning home to the sites of destroyed villages when the land is empty? In some instances, however, the village's former land is now used for Israeli agriculture, and in other instances Israeli Jews now live in former Palestinian homes. Palestinian refugees from the destroyed village of Sheikh Muwwanis, where Tel Aviv University now sits,

have thought of creative solutions for compensation and coexistence. Not wishing to return at the price of destroying Israeli buildings, one refugee suggested that as a form of compensation, his family be given property to live on nearby so that they can visit the site of the village. He proposed that his descendants up to an agreed-on generation receive the right to attend the university for free. What are other creative ways to think about return in situations involving new inhabitants in refugees' homes?

2. Throughout history, liberation for some meant at times dispossession for others. What might a liberation life-giving for *all* the people of Palestine-Israel look like?

3. How has your perception of history shaped how you see the country you live in? Who has been left out of the dominant narrative told in your country's history books? How can that narrative be reshaped to include those voices?

SUGGESTIONS FOR ACTION

1. MCC first came to Palestine in 1949, in response to the refugee crisis brought on by the 1948 war. Learn more about MCC's work and about Palestine-Israel in *What Is Palestine-Israel? Answers to Common Questions* (Herald Press, 2007).

2. For more information on these refugee issues as well as on how Palestinians and Israelis are working together for a shared future of justice and peace, contact the Badil Resource Center for Palestinian Residency and Refugee Rights at www.badil.org and the Zochrot Association at www.nakbainhebrew.org.

3. Plan a Sunday of prayer and advocacy at your church focusing on Palestine-Israel. Include prayers for Palestinians and Israelis—for their security, freedom from violence, and future of peace and reconciliation. Contact MCC's offices in Ottawa (see www.mcc.org/canada/ottawa/) or in Washington, D.C. (see www.mcc.org/us/washington/) for ways to communicate your congregation's prayers and hopes for peace, justice, and reconciliation in Palestine-Israel to government officials.

NOTES

1. For more detailed historical accounts, see two studies by leading Israeli historians: Ilan Pappé's *A History of Modern Palestine: One Land,*

Two Peoples (Cambridge: Cambridge University Press, 2004) and Avi Shlaim's *The Iron Wall: Israel and the Arab World* (New York: W. W. Norton & Company, 1999). Other resources for further learning are listed at the end of this book.

2. Joel Beinin and Lisa Hajjar, *Palestine, Israel and the Arab-Israeli Conflict: A Primer* (Washington, DC: Middle East Research and Information Project, 2001). Available at www.merip.org.

3. Ilan Pappé, *A History of Modern Palestine*, 14.

4. Ilan Pappé, *A History of Modern Palestine*, 36.

5. Rashid Khalidi, *Resurrecting Empire: Western Footprints and America's Perilous Path in the Middle East* (London: I.B. Taurus, 2004), 120.

6. See Ilan Pappé, *A History of Modern Palestine*, 134; and Avi Shlaim, *The Iron Wall*, 35.

7. Avi Shlaim, "The 'New History' of 1948 and the Palestinian Nakba," from the text of a workshop in London, posted at *MIFTAH.org*, March 18, 2004, at www.miftah.org/Display.cfm?DocId=3336&CategoryId=5.

8. Ilan Pappé, *A History of Modern Palestine*, 146.

9. Ilan Pappé, *A History of Modern Palestine*, 139.

10. Meron Benvenisti, *Sacred Landscape: Buried History of the Holy Land Since 1948* (Berkeley: University of California Press, 2001); quoted in Ilan Pappé, *A History of Modern Palestine*, 147.

11. Ilan Pappé, *A History of Modern Palestine*, 198.

12. Ilan Pappé, *A History of Modern Palestine*, 254.

13. Ilan Pappé, *A History of Modern Palestine*, 255.

14. Avi Shlaim, "The 'New History' of 1948 and the Palestinian Nakba."

15. Avi Shlaim, "The 'New History' of 1948 and the Palestinian Nakba."

Chapter 2

Getting Grounded: The Land Belongs to God

Timothy Seidel

The earth is the Lord's, and all that is in it, the world, and those who
who live in it
——Psalm 24:1

One afternoon, on my way into Jerusalem, I noticed that the Israeli military had begun building another portion of the separation barrier inside Bethlehem, right across the street from a hospital. Walking back home from the checkpoint later that night with some friends, I saw that the concrete blocks making up this part of the barrier, nearly thirty feet (nine meters) high, had all been erected. It was a striking and imposing sight.

Just imagine walking down a street, a hospital to your left and this giant wall to your right. My friends and I stopped for a few minutes to talk with a young man who lives in one of the buildings now across the street from the massive wall. He mentioned that he and his family were hoping to add another story to their home. Palestinians routinely add stories to their homes for their children to move into when they grow up and get married. Adding a new floor will now be impossible for this family because the Israeli military has decreed that buildings adjacent to the wall cannot extend higher than the wall, as that would constitute a "security threat" to those on the other side of the wall. In fact, this young man worried, his home might soon be demolished for being too tall as it is now.

If today you passed this stretch of wall, you might notice protest art painted on the concrete slabs. It offers this prophetic exhortation: "Israel, 'Thou shall not steal' still applies. God."

Walls and electrified fences erected by the Israeli military are all-too-common features of the Palestinian landscape. Bridges of friendship and reconciliation are sadly in short supply. The separation barrier has wreaked havoc on Palestinians living under Israeli occupation. Livelihoods have been disrupted, families separated, Palestinian farmers cut off from their land and often forced to watch their harvest rot in the fields. Others see their trees uprooted to make way for the walls and fences of the separation barrier. This ongoing experience of dispossession exacerbates an already bleak economic reality for Palestinians in the Occupied Territories, where unemployment figures run as high as sixty percent.

Some theological readings of Scripture justify the dispossession Palestinians have faced over the past six decades. Specifically, Christian Zionist theologies argue that, as God has given the land to the Jewish people forever, Palestinians should be content with second-class status at best—if not moved, willingly or by force, from the land. Even many Christians who would balk at the more explicitly violent versions of Christian Zionist theology, meanwhile, struggle with how to relate biblical land promises to the current Palestinian-Israeli conflict. "Didn't God promise this land to Abraham, Isaac, Jacob, and their descendants?," people often ask. "Didn't God give this land to the Jews?"

How can different parts of Scripture be brought into conversation with the contemporary realities in Palestine-Israel? How do Old Testament land promises, the narratives of conquest in Joshua and Judges, prophetic visions of security in the land, and apocalyptic material relate? Can the Bible be read in ways that do not justify violence and dispossession but that instead support struggles for reconciliation founded on joint Palestinian-Israeli work for nonviolence and justice?

What, to use the apt phrase coined by Marlin Jeschke, is the "salvation geography" proclaimed in Scripture? Jeschke helpfully outlines the important questions that this book seeks to address, with particular reference to the Palestinian-Israeli conflict: "What does it mean to receive the promise of land, to inherit it, to possess it, to be exiled from it, to return to it, to steward it, above all to sanctify it?"[1]

Not only this chapter but also several subsequent ones wrestle with such questions. In this chapter, I begin to tackle them by offering an overview of a biblical theology of land, a way to read Scripture's different strands on the question of land as a whole. The biblical theology of land I sketch has been influenced by the groundbreaking work of Palestinian Christian theologians and church leaders such as Elias Chacour, Naim Ateek, and Mitri Raheb, Christians who think and pray with the Bible amid the Palestinian context and for whom the gospel message energizes and sustains commitment to justice and reconciliation.

THE LAND BELONGS TO GOD

The starting point for any Christian thinking about the land of Palestine-Israel (or any land) should be Genesis 1: God is the Creator. From the very beginning Scripture testifies to a God who reveals God's self as Creator and Sustainer. As Creator and Sustainer, God is also the Provider of order who, even in the Garden of Eden, establishes a framework for right relationships and right living in the land God provides. This divine framework is one in which humans as creatures relate to God the Creator with trust and obedience.

From the beginning of Scripture until the end, the message is the same: the land belongs to God. In Leviticus 25, we see this explicitly stated in the discussion of the Sinai covenant. There the people are told, "The land shall not be sold in perpetuity, for the land is mine; with me you are but aliens and tenants" (25:23). The confession that the land belongs to God, that humans are but tenants on the land that God provides, means all human claims to land are relativized.

And if the land belongs to God, then not only are all claims to the land relativized but violent attempts to dominate and control land can properly be understood as idolatrous. To position ourselves in a place of exclusive domination or control over the land is to set ourselves up as gods, claiming prerogatives that rightly only belong to the Creator.

If we are but tenants on the land, we must live in the land on God's terms. Leviticus 25 spells out that our obligations to God involve living out the liberation and justice bound up in the year of "Jubilee." "You shall proclaim liberty throughout the land to all its inhabitants," God tells the people (25:10), with debts forgiven and persons who have lost land through indebtedness allowed to return to the land. Through the Jubilee practice of justice and righteousness, God's people receive security: "You shall observe my statutes and faithfully keep my ordinances, so that you may live on the land securely" (25:18).

Deuteronomy records God making a similar call on God's people to combine life in the land with just living: "So now, Israel, give heed to the statutes and ordinances that I am teaching you to observe, so that you may live to enter and occupy the land that the Lord, the God of your ancestors, is giving you" (4:1). God's people must observe the commandments "diligently," Deuteronomy continues, "for this," God says, "will show your wisdom and discernment to the peoples, who, when they hear all these statutes, will say, 'Surely this great nation is a wise and discerning people!'" (4:6).

Diligent attention to God's law will be the wellspring of Israel's life, the discipline that shapes its unique theological witness. Israel will become a "great nation" and a "wise and discerning people" by virtue of its ethical character and its attentiveness to God's ultimate sovereignty. Israel's peoplehood is not defined so much by its possession of land as by its faithful witness to the God to whom the land finally belongs.

In the vision of reconciliation as right living delineated by God's instructions to his people at Sinai, right relationship with God is inextricably linked not only to a right relationship with the land but also to right relationships with others in the land. To place ourselves in positions of domination and control over others and over the land is, again, to commit idolatry; it is an act of taking land as an exclusive possession rather than receiving it as a gift from God.

Throughout Israel's existence in the land, prophetic voices call the people to obedience to the Torah, to the Sinai covenant, the blueprint for right living and right relationships. Jesus locates himself in this same tradition when he claims to bring good news to the poor and to the captive (Luke 4:18). Deuteronomy well expresses this prophetic insistence on the just treatment of those most marginalized by society—the widow, the orphan, the resident alien:

> You shall not deprive a resident alien or an orphan of justice; you shall not take a widow's garment in pledge. Remember that you were a slave in Egypt and the Lord your God redeemed you from there; therefore I command you to do this.
>
> When you reap your harvest in your field and forget a sheaf in the field, you shall not go back to get it; it shall be left for the alien, the orphan, and the widow, so that the Lord your God may bless you in all your undertakings. When you beat your olive trees, do not strip what is left; it shall be for the alien, the orphan, and the widow.
>
> When you gather the grapes of your vineyard, do not glean what is left; it shall be for the alien, the orphan, and the widow. Remember that you were a slave in the land of Egypt; therefore I am commanding you to do this. (Deut. 24:17-22)

The poor, the oppressed, the stranger in the land—these persons function in Scripture as a constant reminder to God's people of where they once came from, who they once were, a reminder of God's abiding concern for the "least of these":

> When an alien resides with you in your land, you shall not oppress the alien. The alien who resides with you shall be to you as the citizen among you; you shall love the alien as yourself, for you were aliens in the land of Egypt: I am the Lord your God. (Lev. 19:33-34)

> For the Lord your God is God of gods and Lord of lords, the great God, mighty and awesome, who is not partial and takes no bribe, who executes justice for the orphan and the widow, who loves the stranger, providing them food and clothing. You shall also love the stranger, for you were strangers in the land of Egypt. (Deut. 10:17-19)

God's people are to show compassion for the weak, the poor, sojourners, newcomers/resident aliens (*ger*) precisely because Israel knows each of these positions firsthand. Remembering that they were once strangers or aliens in Egypt, God's people are motivated to keep the law. Remembering that they were once aliens and strangers also helps them check any desire to control land in ways that dispossess others. God particularly denounces the amassing of property at the expense of others, those "who join house to house, who add field to field, until there is room for no one but you" (Isa. 5:8). The prophet Micah speaks similarly:

> Alas for those who devise wickedness
> and evil deeds on their beds!
> When the morning dawns, they perform it,
> because it is in their power.
> They covet fields, and seize them;
> houses, and take them away;
> they oppress householder and house,
> people and their inheritance. (Mic. 2:1-3)

The Hebrew prophetic tradition constantly challenges the powerful who join house to house, field to field, forcing others off of the land. The prophet Isaiah appropriates the Jubilee tradition from Leviticus in service of a vision of liberation for the captive, for those marginalized on the land:

> The spirit of the Lord God is upon me
> because the Lord has anointed me;
> he has sent me to bring good news to the oppressed,
> to bind up the brokenhearted,
> to proclaim liberty to the captives,
> and release to the prisoners;
> to proclaim the year of the Lord's favor. (Isa. 61:1-2)

The reiteration of Isaiah's proclamation in Jesus' inaugural sermon in the gospel of Luke (4:18-19) indicates that the tradition of subversive good news links Old and New Testaments, the gospel of justice and liberation being definitive for both the Jewish and Christian traditions.[2]

MUTUAL BLESSING

Our reading of Scripture so far points to a particular understanding of God, an understanding of God as one who works for the liberation and landed security of the dispossessed and the marginalized. For Palestinian Christian theologians, the question of "Who is God?" is crucial. For Naim Ateek, a Palestinian Anglican priest and theologian, a central theological question is how the church, "without rejecting any part of the Bible," can "adequately relate the core of the biblical message—its concept of God—to Palestinians."[3] For Palestinian Christians, Ateek continues, "the existence of God is not in doubt. What has been seriously questioned is the nature and character of God. What is God really like?"[4] All too familiar with readings of Scripture that justify Palestinian dispossession, Palestinian Christians ask how it will speak a liberating word to them, how it will reveal a God who cares for the dispossessed. The key question for Palestinian Christians, according to Ateek, is "whether what is being read in the Bible is the Word of *God* to them and whether it reflects the nature, will, and purpose of *God* for them."[5]

For Ateek, the Bible must be read in the light of God's revelation in Jesus Christ if it is to be good news for Palestinians (and for others). Jesus, Ateek says, is "the true hermeneutic, the key to understanding the Bible, and beyond the Bible to the understanding of the action of God throughout history. In other words, the *Word* of God incarnate in Jesus the Christ interprets for us the *word* of God in the Bible."[6] The land promises to Abraham and his descendants, the conquest narratives, the prophetic call to do justice on the land—the contemporary reception of all parts of Scripture, according to Ateek, must be determined by the church's confession of Jesus as the definitive revelation of God's identity and mission: "The revelation of God, God's nature, purpose, and will as revealed in Christ, becomes the criterion by which Christians can measure the validity and authority of the biblical message for their lives."[7]

Ateek identifies the story of Naboth's vineyard in 1 Kings 21 as a key text for Palestinian Christians. The story of Naboth, set up on false charges by the royal court so King Ahab and Queen Jezebel could take possession of his vineyard, reveals God's "uncompromising concern for justice" and the tenacity of God's ethical law, a law that, "championed by the Prophets, operated impartially: every person's rights, property, and very life were under divine protection." The story shows God intervening "to defend the poor, the weak, and the defenseless."[8]

Doing justice and practicing righteousness in the land are, Ateek stresses, imperative for secure life in the land. Because the earth is the Lord's, "Those who want to live on the land . . . must obey the owner of the land. Disobedience to God defiles the land, violates its sacred character, and incurs the unequivocal loss of the land."[9] The Hebrew prophets shatter tribalistic and exclusivist understandings of God, describing God instead as a "God of justice and righteousness who demands ethical living of all nations."[10]

One can trace a development of the concept of God in the Old Testament from one of God as only for the people of Israel to one of God as sovereign over the whole world, a development shaped by Israel's exile from the land. "Our understanding of God today obliges us to conclude that the God who was perceived by the Israelites as the God who owned 'the land of Canaan' is none other than the God whom we have come to know as the God who owns the whole world," writes Ateek. This does not mean that the particularity of God's calling of the Israelites is no longer important. Quite the opposite: "The land that God has chosen at one particular time in history for one particular people is now perceived as a paradigm, a model, for God's concern for every people and every land."[11] By responding to the God of life and love by establishing and maintaining right relationships in the land, God's people become a means for the mutual blessing of all nations.

The exile of God's people from the land opened Israel to understand God as sovereign over all lands, over all of creation. Living in exile, the people had to adjust their land-bound concept of God. It was in the Babylonian captivity that "the Israelites had to learn that God was not confined to 'their' land."[12] Exile, Ateek stresses, taught God's people that their "relationship with God did not depend on being on the land. God without the land is infinitely more important than the land without God."[13]

Ateek's argument here meshes well with the late John Howard Yoder's description of the people of God, who, being radically reliant on God, are "not in charge" of history and whose communal life is defined not by a particular land but by living out a faithful witness to God's reign in all lands.[14] The prophet Jeremiah's exhortation to "seek the welfare of the city where I have sent you into exile" (29:7) becomes, for the people Israel and for the church, a paradigmatic call—a mission to do justice and practice righteousness in all corners of the earth.

As strangers in Babylon, aliens in exile, God's people learn that they can sanctify the land of their exile by following God's commandments in exile, thereby seeking the well-being, the *shalom*, of the cities of their exile. Whether in the promised land or in exile, God's people are strangers and aliens, tenants on the land God graciously gives, and are called to do justice, to show mercy as they have been shown mercy.

CONCLUSION

Latin American theologian Gustavo Gutiérrez has emphasized at length that God is first and foremost the God of life.[15] God's fundamental character as the good giver of life deepens our understanding of God's attributes. God is life as God liberates. God is holy as God does justice. God is faithful as God makes a covenant to bring blessing and life. Professing faith in the God of life means a rejection of the death-dealing forces of poverty, oppression, dehumanization, and the structures of violence and sin that produce them.

In terms of a theology of land, this means rejecting policies, practices, and ideologies that dispossess others and exclude people from the blessings of landed security. The land of Palestine-Israel is sadly replete with stories of persons being excluded from security in the land and dispossessed of land. But there are also many Palestinians and Israelis—Christian, Muslim, and Jewish—who remember that the God of life calls upon God's creatures to do justice in the land, to care for those who are marginalized, to receive the gift of land as an opportunity for mutual blessing, not to grab hold of it as an exclusive possession. Both stories—the story of dispossession and walls, and the story of bridges of reconciliation built through joint work for justice—run through the remainder of this book.

QUESTIONS FOR DISCUSSION

1. Explore and discuss the Bible's approach to land, considering the responsibilities that accompany the land and other people living in the land (Lev. 19:33, 34; Deut. 10:17-19, 24:17-22). Consider refugee experiences throughout the world, past and present. What does Scripture say about exile and the longing for

home? How can the Bible and history be read to build a future of just peace throughout Palestine-Israel and the world?

2. Colossians 3:9-11 stresses that when we align ourselves with the image of our Creator, we find equality between all people (Jew and Greek, circumcised and uncircumcised, slave and free). How can this call to align ourselves with our Creator shape our perspective of the situation in Palestine-Israel and how we should see and love the "Other?"

3. According to Israel's Law of Return, any Jew can come to live as a citizen in the state of Israel. Some even receive financial benefits (such as free plane tickets, free housing, tax exemptions, free medical insurance, and language study). Compare this with Israel's refusal to allow Palestinian refugees who wish to live in peace with their neighbors to return (as called for in UN General Assembly Resolution 194). What is Israel's responsibility to the Palestinian refugees? What is the international community's responsibility to the Palestinian refugees?

SUGGESTIONS FOR ACTION

1. View the MCC video *Children of the Nakba* with your church or small group to learn more about the realities of the Nakba for both Palestinians and Israelis (available from your local MCC office or online at www.mcc.org/catalog).

2. Churches for Middle East Peace (CMEP) is a coalition of churches and church-related organizations that works for a future of justice and peace for Palestinians and Israelis alike. Look on the CMEP website (www.cmep.org) for ideas about how to urge your government to work for justice, peace, and reconciliation in Palestine-Israel.

NOTES

1. See Marlin Jeschke, *Rethinking Holy Land: A Study in Salvation Geography* (Scottdale, Pa.: Herald Press, 2005), 23. Jeschke's study is an accessible yet thorough overview of how land is treated in the Bible.

2. For a fuller account of the place of the Jubilee in Scripture, see "The Implications of Jubilee," chapter 3 of John Howard Yoder's *The Politics of Jesus: Vicit Agnus Noster* (Grand Rapids: Wm. B. Eerdmans, 1994).

3. Naim Stifan Ateek, *Justice and Only Justice: A Palestinian Theology*

of Liberation (Maryknoll, N.Y.: Orbis Books, 1989), 78.

4. Ateek, *Justice and Only Justice*, 78.

5. Ateek, *Justice and Only Justice*, 79.

6. Ateek, *Justice and Only Justice*, 80.

7. Ateek, *Justice and Only Justice*, 81.

8. Ateek, *Justice and Only Justice*, 88.

9. Ateek, *Justice and Only Justice*, 105.

10. Ateek, *Justice and Only Justice*, 96.

11. Ateek, *Justice and Only Justice*, 108.

12. Ateek, *Justice and Only Justice*, 110.

13. Ateek, *Justice and Only Justice*, 111.

14. See chapter 9, "On Not Being in Charge," in John Howard Yoder, *The Jewish-Christian Schism Revisited*, ed. Michael G. Cartwright and Peter Ochs (Grand Rapids: Wm. B. Eerdmans, 2003).

15. Gustavo Gutierréz, *The God of Life* (Maryknoll, N.Y.: Orbis Books, 1991).

Chapter 3

Abraham's Promised Land

Dan Epp-Tiessen

"Then the Lord appeared to Abram, and said, 'To your offspring I will give this land.'"
—Genesis 12:7

Two teenage Jewish boys in the Old City of Jerusalem unapologetically assert that the land of Palestine and the city of Jerusalem belong to them and the Jewish people. This is because God gave the land to Abraham and his descendents. Therefore, Jewish claims to the land supersede the claims of other residents, even if these other residents have lived in the land for over a thousand years. Interestingly, these boys arrived in Jerusalem only a few months ago from New York.[1]

In the West Bank the fertile Jordan Valley is now almost entirely occupied by Israeli farms. Throughout the West Bank it is difficult to travel more than ten miles without encountering yet another Israeli settlement, many newly constructed and strategically located on a hilltop. The strategy seems obvious—gradually to take over more and more land and water until the Palestinians are dispossessed and lose their economic base and to build up Israeli-controlled areas in such a way that a viable, contiguous Palestinian state becomes impossible. Many of the settlers are deeply religious and see themselves as on a mission to claim the land God promised to Abraham and his descendents.

"Christian Zionism seeks to declare the truth of God's Word that bequeaths to the people of Israel the land of Canaan as an everlasting possession," declares the International Christian Embassy of Jerusalem. "This promise was made by God to Abraham some four thousand years ago (Gen. 13:14-18)."[2] Evangelical Christian groups in North America proclaim on their websites and in their advertisements for tours to Israel that God has promised the land to the Jewish people. Therefore, Christians must support Israeli actions to acquire the entire land of Palestine for Jews. As a result, Christians deny or overlook the destruction of Palestinian farms, the bulldozing of Palestinian homes, and other means used to dispossess Palestinians of land and resources.

GOD'S PROMISES TO ABRAHAM

The situations described above have direct connections to the Bible. In the book of Genesis God repeatedly promises to grant the land to Abraham and his descendants (12:7; 13:14-17; 15:18-21; 26:3-4; 28:13; 35:12). Later passages frequently refer to this same promise as the basis on which God leads the Israelites into the land (e.g. Exod. 6:8; Deut. 1:8; 6:10). Today many Jews and Christians base their convictions about the current situation in Palestine on these promises. God has granted the land of Palestine to the Jewish people as an inalienable possession. Therefore, morally questionable practices used by Israelis to occupy the land can be overlooked or rationalized because these actions serve to fulfill God's ancient promises.

God's promise to Abraham stands at the beginning of the Jewish people's experience with the land. For some 1,400 years Israelites/Jews enjoyed the privilege of living in the land, from about 1250 BCE until 135 CE, when they were driven out by the Romans. Even when Jews were living in diaspora for centuries, they always maintained a powerful spiritual attachment to the land. The favorable political conditions in the twentieth century for establishing the state of Israel and returning to the land have led many Jews to believe that they now have a religious obligation to claim and occupy the whole land, even if inhabited by another people. Thus God's promise of the land to Abraham and his descendants has become a basis for denying Palestinian claims to the land, for justifying strategies to push Palestinians off the land, or for making their life in Palestine so miserable that they will leave "voluntarily."

Many Western Christians also put much stock in God's promise to Abraham, and some Christians support the building of Jewish settlements on land confiscated from Palestinian communities. Christians rarely raise a voice when the Israeli military bulldozes Palestinian homes or when Israel builds an ugly impenetrable "security" wall reaching up to thirty feet (nine meters) high deep into West Bank Palestinian territory, demolishing homes in the process and cutting off Palestinian communities and farmers from their land.

One mile from where I wrote this chapter, backhoes and cranes are putting finishing touches on the wall around Bethlehem, a Palestinian city of some 60,000 people. The city is now enclosed, a massive steel gate and huge military checkpoint guarding the entry and exit point. Foreign tourists are allowed to come and go, to make their pilgrimage to the place of Jesus' birth, but 60,000 Palestinians are enclosed in a ghetto, with only a few able to acquire the necessary permits to travel to nearby Jerusalem or other parts of the West Bank. Outside Bethlehem and its confining wall, numerous tall cranes preside over construction sites busily building more housing for Jewish families, enticing them to move ever deeper into West Bank Palestinian territory.

Many Christians view Israel's occupation of the West Bank and its acquisition of ever more land at Palestinian expense as ways in which Israel is fulfilling its biblical mandate to re-inhabit the land God promised Abraham. Is this really what God wants? Does God's promise to Abraham justify Israeli practices that inflict massive hardship on Palestinians? Perhaps there are other ways of interpreting the ongoing significance of God's promises. Since the promises made to Abraham and his descendants play a crucial role in the biblical story, perhaps the place to begin is by examining these promises in the context of this larger story.

The biblical story begins with God creating an amazing and wonderful world, but quickly things go wrong. In Genesis 3 the first humans eat of the forbidden fruit and the power of sin is unleashed. In the next story, Cain murders his brother Abel, and before long human sin has reached such epic proportions that God resorts to drastic measures. A massive flood engulfs the world,

but when all is said and done, God admits that the flood has not
eliminated the human inclination to sin (Gen. 8:21). God's pes-
simistic assessment of humanity is quickly born out by the story
of how humankind asserts its pride and arrogance by seeking to
build the massive tower and city of Babel (Gen. 11:1-9).

After Genesis 11, there is a major shift in the story, as God
adopts a new strategy for dealing with the problem of human
sinfulness so prominent in the earlier chapters. God calls Abraham and Sarah. This call is accompanied by important promises.
God promises to make of them a great nation, to bless them, and
to make them a blessing, so that in them all the families of the
earth might receive blessing (12:1-3).

At this point God does not yet say anything about the land.
More important than the land is God's new venture of creating a
covenant people. In the rest of the Bible this becomes God's strategy for dealing with the sinful human condition—the formation
of a people who experience God's salvation, are entrusted with
God's revelation, and are called to establish a community whose
character reflects the nature and will of God. God's promises and
special blessing will accompany this people, but the blessing is
not just an end in itself. Its purpose is to empower God's people
to bless the rest of the world (Gen. 12:3; 22:18; 26:4). Instead of
giving up on the fallen humanity portrayed in much of Genesis
1-11, God calls Abraham and Sarah to found a people who will
channel God's blessing and salvation to this fallen humanity.

This is the proper context for understanding God's repeated
promise of land to Abraham and his descendants. The land
promise does not stand on its own but plays a key role in God's
much larger agenda of creating a covenant people who practice
justice and righteousness and channel divine blessing to others
(Gen. 18:18-19). In the ancient world it was not possible for a people to survive without a territory of their own. Since God's project was to create a people, God needed to provide a land where
they could flourish and live out their calling to establish a unique
identity.

When Christians and Jews today cite God's promise of land
as justification for expanding Jewish settlements on Palestinian
land or destroying Palestinian homes, we must ask if such actions are really in keeping with God's intentions for promising
the land to Abraham and his descendants. What kinds of actions

and policies in the land channel God's blessing to other peoples, and what kinds of actions bring pain and hardship?

It is striking to observe how Abraham, the first recipient of the land promise, provides a model for how to live peacefully in the land alongside its Canaanite inhabitants. Abraham wanders through the land with his herds—he displaces no one and no one seeks to harm him. Apparently the land has enough space and resources for all who seek to live there. The Canaanite priest Melchizedek blesses Abraham, then Abraham gives him a tithe (14:18-20). When God wishes to destroy the notoriously wicked cities of Sodom and Gomorrah, Abraham does not rejoice. Instead, he drives a hard bargain with God in a futile effort to save them (18:22-33). When Abraham lies about Sarah's identity, claiming that she is his sister, Abraham's unfaithfulness brings suffering rather than blessing on others (20:17-18; cf. 12:17).

The Philistine King Abimelech takes Sarah into his harem, but when God reveals Sarah's true identity to him, Abimelech acts with utmost integrity. He acknowledges Abraham's God, showers Abraham with gifts, and even invites him to settle in Philistine territory (20:1-18). Abraham prays for the king and consequently Abimelech's family is healed (20:17-18), illustrating Abraham's power to channel blessing. When Sarah dies, Abraham does not cite God's promise of land as justification for seizing a burial plot. Rather, he negotiates and is careful to purchase a burial plot legally and pay the full price (23:3-16). Abraham's life in the land is both a model of peaceful coexistence and an illustration of how to mediate divine blessing to others.[3]

Abraham's story provides a striking contrast to what we find later in the book of Joshua. In Joshua the model for living in the land as recipients of God's promise is to engage in genocide and ethnic cleansing so that no Canaanites are left in the land. (For more on Joshua see chapter 4.) Abraham chooses the route of peaceful relationships, which leads to peace and well-being for himself as well as for the indigenous inhabitants of the land.

THE STORY OF ISRAEL AND THE LAND

At the heart of Israel's possession of the land in the Old Testament stands a paradox. On the one hand, God's promise of the land is unconditional. On the other hand, the land is granted conditionally. Since the land ultimately belongs to God and Israel only receives it as a gift, life in the land must be lived on God's terms. Hence, God repeatedly threatens Israel with loss of the land if she is unfaithful and if she does not establish a just society in the land (see Lev. 26:31-34; Deut. 28:62-64; Jer. 7:1-15; Amos 6:1-7).

The land can be lost because God does not promise or grant the land as an end in itself. God's purpose is to make possible the formation of a covenant people who will establish a just, righteous, and faithful society in the land. If Israel does not live up to this calling, then she will forfeit the land. The two poles of this paradox are never resolved or harmonized in the Old Testament, as each contributes its unique emphasis. God is unconditionally committed to Israel as a people living in the land. Israel's life in the land is dependent on faithfulness, and the land can be lost.

In fact, the land was lost. The Bible interprets the destruction of Jerusalem, and the exile of many Jews to Babylon in 587 BCE, as Israel's loss of the land because of its unfaithfulness. One significant impact of the Babylonian Exile was that many Jews learned to live without the land. After 538 BCE, when the Jewish exiles in Babylon were allowed to return to the land, many chose to remain in Babylon because life there had become comfortable. Increasingly, Jewish people dispersed across the Mediterranean world, most searching for better economic prospects than life in the land could offer. While faithful Jews maintained a strong connection to the land of Palestine, they also learned to live faithfully as Jews in diaspora outside the land. This adaptation is one of the main reasons Judaism did not collapse when the Romans expelled virtually all Jews from Palestine in 135 CE and the land was lost once again.

In the centuries that followed, Jews established strong communities across western and eastern Europe, North Africa, and various locations in the Middle East. Vicious persecution at the hands of Christians often forced Jews to seek out new lands where they could find some level of security and well-being. Judaism achieved a measure of peace with living outside the land, no doubt in part because Jews were not permitted to return to Palestine. While Judaism always fostered a strong attachment to the land, there was no large-scale movement to return to Palestine and claim the land promised to Abraham. Many Jews believed that such a return would not occur until the arrival of the Messiah.

The rise of Zionism in the late nineteenth century brought significant changes in Jewish belief. Theodor Herzl, founder of modern Zionism, argued that Jews needed their own homeland as a safe haven from ever-present anti-Judaism in Europe. Initially Zionism was a tough sell, because many secular Jews believed that Jewish security lay in assimilation, while most religious Jews believed that only the Messiah would restore them to the land. Bolstered by ongoing anti-Judaism in Europe, the Zionist movement convinced a growing number of Jews and non-Jews that a Jewish homeland in Palestine was necessary.

The Holocaust greatly strengthened this conviction, as it demonstrated all-too frighteningly how cruel the world could be to Jews, and how vulnerable Jews could be even in a supposedly civilized western society. Given that Jews had for centuries lived in tenuous circumstances as minority communities in the West, the Holocaust enhanced enormously the appeal of creating a Jewish state where Jews would be the majority and could control their own affairs.

The Jewish state that Zionists envisioned seemed to promise a safe haven from persecution. Horror at the slaughter of the Holocaust also increased Western support for Zionism, and, as Israeli historian Benny Morris notes, "the need for a sanctuary for the world's oppressed Jews was made clear to the community of nations." Not surprisingly, "hundreds of thousands of Jewish survivors" of the Holocaust "refused to remain anywhere near the killing fields," but "Western European countries and the United States were unwilling to take them in, and the Zionists wanted them in Palestine."[4] Palestinians, understandably, resented what they saw as a Western attempt to atone for the guilt of the Holocaust at the expense of Palestinian rights.

The Zionist movement had always highlighted the vulnerability of Jewish existence in the Diaspora and even called for a "negation of the Diaspora" (*shelilat ha-galut*). Both before and after 1948, Zionist and Israeli leaders contrasted Diaspora weakness with Israeli strength, emphasizing that only the latter could ensure that atrocities like the Holocaust would never happen again. For many Israelis, the Holocaust provides a definitive lesson that the Jewish people must rely on their own strength in their own land. Israeli sociologist Baruch Kimmerling observes that much of Israeli society perceives the "Gentile world, Arab and non-Arab," as hostile to Jews, "its self-evident and permanent goal of annihilating the Jewish people" gruesomely demonstrated by the Holocaust.[5]

The call for Jews to return to Palestine to claim God's promise of land to Abraham, then, was not a significant feature of Jewish belief for many centuries. It came to the fore as modern Zionism gained momentum, and only in the last century has it played an increasing role in justifying the settling of a land that was already populated by Palestinian Arabs.

Only quite recently have Jews and Christians begun appealing to God's promise of land to Abraham as justification for pushing Palestinians off the land. It is by no means inevitable that Jews and Christians should legitimate current Israeli expansion on the basis of biblical promises. Before the twentieth century, few Christians supported a Jewish return to the land by appealing to the promises to Abraham, and for most of the last two thousand years Jewish people have lived faithfully without claiming that they have a divine obligation to return to Palestine and claim all the land promised to Abraham and his descendants. Even today many Christians and Jews are deeply troubled by appeals to God's promise of land to Abraham as a justification for actions that dispossess Palestinians.

For many Jews today, the state of Israel functions as a safe homeland for Jewish people from around the world. The horrible history of persecution of the Jews, far too much of it perpetrated by Christians, demonstrates, in their minds, the need for such a safe haven. Christians should appreciate the Jewish desire for a safe haven, even as we raise questions about whether or not safety can be secured through policies and practices of dispossessing another people. Christians should also recognize that the made-in-the-West problem of anti-Judaism has been partly resolved on the backs of Palestinians, including Palestinian Christians, who have been forced to surrender control of their communities and much of their homeland in the interests of creating a safe homeland for Jewish immigrants to Palestine. After World War II, Western nations like Canada and the U.S. were very sympathetic to Jewish refugees, as long as most of them landed on the shores of Palestine and not on our shores.

Christians ought to acknowledge both the spiritual and practical significance of the land of Palestine for the Jewish people and should appreciate the deep spiritual attachment which Palestinians have to the same land. Both Israelis and Palestinians are called to live justly and to practice righteousness in the land. As Western Christians, we should support the efforts of those Israelis and Palestinians who practice hospitality instead of expulsion, who plant trees rather than uproot them, and who extend hands in friendship rather than to strike.

THE NEW TESTAMENT AND THE LAND

Land was a burning issue during the time of Jesus. It was a central theme in Jewish Scripture, from God's promise of the land to Abraham to prophetic texts which anticipated the coming of God's kingdom that would liberate the land from foreign oppression and all forms of injustice and uncleanness. The Roman occupation of Palestine and the heavy burdens shouldered by the Jewish population fueled a longing for God's intervention and the establishment of God's reign in the land. Jesus was sympathetic to the suffering of his people, but in significant ways he broke with many of the contemporary hopes regarding the land. Jesus proclaimed the arrival of God's kingdom, but this kingdom had little to do with the establishment of a Jewish state and the defeat of Gentile nations.

Many Jewish hopes had become centered on Jerusalem, God's holy city. Jesus respected the temple as God's house, but he did not revere Jerusalem like most pious Jews did, nor did he foresee a significant role for Jerusalem in a future earthly kingdom. Instead, Jesus proclaimed the destruction of both temple and city (Mark 13:1-2; Matt. 24:1-2; Luke 21:5-6:20-24). Jesus claimed to be the Messiah, but his claims had little to do with presiding over a restored Jewish state. Jesus sought to gather a community of people who would be faithful to God and the new things God was doing in the world, but this community was not by definition linked to the land of Palestine.

At the core of Jesus' proclamation stands the breaking in of God's kingdom. God was offering humanity salvation in the form of healing, forgiveness of sin, defeat of evil and demonic forces, and restoration to wholeness. Jesus invited people to participate in God's reign by accepting the grace God offered, by forsaking sinful lifestyles, and by joining a new community committed to a life of grace, righteousness, justice, and peace. The great commission and many other texts stress that God invites all persons to commit their lives to Jesus and become part of the new people of God (Matt. 28:18-20).

Jesus was certainly aware of literal interpretations of God's promises of land, but he chose to go in a different direction. Instead of appealing to a literal fulfillment of God's promise of land to Abraham, Jesus universalized the promise. In the Beatitudes he quotes Psalm 37:11, which states that the meek will inherit the land (meaning literal land in Palestine). Jesus paraphrases this verse to read "Blessed are the meek, for they will inherit the earth" (Matt. 5:5). Jesus asserts that God's concern extends far beyond the land of Palestine, and when God's reign comes in all its fullness, then the meek will inherit the entire world.

In the Old Testament the land is important as the primary sphere of God's engagement with God's people. In the New Testament there is a significant shift. The land continues to be significant, but primarily because it serves as the launching pad for God's activity in the broader world. This is particularly evident in the book of Acts. The gospel takes root in Jerusalem, and Paul makes repeated trips back to Jerusalem, but from there the gospel spreads to the broader world, until the book closes with Paul proclaiming the good news of Jesus in Rome, the heart of the empire.

The early followers of Jesus carried on his reinterpretation of the Old Testament land promises. The New Testament writers do not speak of the establishment of a Jewish state as being significant for the kingdom of God, nor do they mention a return of Jews to Palestine from the diaspora. Paul's ministry, for example, focuses not on the national restoration of the Jewish people but on establishing small communities of people across the Roman empire who commit their lives to Christ and his way.

Paul in particular seeks to discern the significance of God's promises to Abraham in light of God's new act of salvation in Jesus Christ. Paul has high regard for the special privileges granted to the Jewish people, but he does not list the land as one of these (Rom. 9:4-5). Paul refers to Abraham as an important ancestor for both Jews and Christians, focusing specifically on Abraham's faith. He concludes that all persons possessing similar faith are the true descendants of Abraham (Rom. 4:11-12; cf. 9:6-8; Gal. 3:6-9). This means that Christians, both Jewish and Gentile, are the true heirs of God's promises to Abraham (Rom. 4:13-14).

Paul cites the important promise that through Abraham all nations will be blessed (Gal. 3:8-9,14). He is convinced that God is now fulfilling this promise by offering salvation to the nations through Jesus Christ. Already in the Old Testament the promise of land is not an end in itself but is part of God's larger purpose to create a faithful people and offer blessing to the nations of the world. Paul's use of the Abraham story continues this trajectory. Concern for the land of Palestine drops out of the picture as Paul focuses on two other features: the blessing that is now made available through Jesus Christ and the new people of God who are Abraham's descendants by faith.

On one occasion Paul does refers to God's promise of land to Abraham, but he reinterprets the promise in two significant ways (Rom. 4:13). First, Paul asserts that the heirs of this promise are all those who are righteous by faith; second, Paul stresses that the promise to Abraham is a promise to inherit the world. Paul universalizes the land in the same way that Jesus does, because he too believes that God's kingdom is not linked to one particular land but will encompass the whole world.

The New Testament focuses on the universal reign of God, so there is no concern for the establishment of a Jewish state in Palestine, even though this was an important concern among Jesus' contemporaries. However, the universalizing of the land does not mean that God's kingdom is purely spiritual and divorced from earthly realities. Rather, it means that God's expectations regarding justice, righteousness, and faithfulness in the land are now extended to include the entire world. The New Testament understanding of God's plan of salvation means that God's promise of the land to Abraham was an important but temporary stage in God's plans for the world. The land was an important gift to the Israelite people because it was of vital importance during a certain period in the history of salvation. Without the land, the Israelites would not have survived and would not have been able to establish a unique identity as God's covenant people. The coming of Jesus Christ, however, inaugurates a new era of salvation. God's plans and purposes now encompass the entire world and all of humanity.

As contemporary Christians, it is not our role to dictate how Jewish people interpret the biblical promises of land. However, we need not be overly preoccupied with the state of Israel as fulfillment of God's promise of the land to Abraham. We can freely recognize Israel's importance for many Jews, but theologically our concern should be that such a state, like all states, practice justice and righteousness, welcome back refugees, and bring an end to practices and policies that strip others of their land. The New Testament demonstrates that God's salvation has been offered to all nations and that God's concern now encompasses all lands. Thus as Christians we must affirm that God is just as concerned with the welfare of Palestinians as the welfare of Jews. To assert that Israelis are called by God to occupy all of Palestine, even if this means pushing Palestinians off the land, is to promote an agenda Jesus and the early church deliberately rejected.

The land of Palestine is certainly the object of God's special concern, as is any part of the world God has created. Israelis and Palestinians are God's children, equally loved. Because both now find themselves in the same land, they have a calling to learn how to share the land, to live as neighbors, and to practice justice. Our beliefs and actions as Christians should serve to promote such harmony.

QUESTIONS FOR DISCUSSION

1. What have you been taught or heard from other Christians about Israel's right to the land? How do these things fit with the ideas and interpretations offered in this chapter?

2. What relevance might the model of Abraham's life in the land have for current realities in Palestine-Israel?

3. What might God's promise of the land to Abraham and his descendants mean for a Jewish survivor of the *Shoah* (Holocaust) contemplating her future in 1945? What might God's promise of the land to Abraham mean for a Palestinian Christian living in the West Bank in the twenty-first century? Or to a Palestinian Muslim in a refugee camp in Lebanon? How expansive and inclusive are God's promises?

SUGGESTIONS FOR ACTION

1. Think of appropriate ways to respond when you hear Christians state that Israel has a right to take over the entire land of Palestine because God promised the land to Abraham and his descendants.

2. Pray that Christians will be discerning and faithful in their application of biblical texts to the Israeli-Palestinian conflict.

NOTES

1. This story is told by Gary M. Burge, *Whose Land? Whose Promise? What Christians Are Not Being Told about Israel and the Palestinians* (Cleveland, Oh.: Pilgrim Press, 2003), 68-69.

2. International Christian Embassy Jerusalem website; "Foundations of Christian Zionism: Biblical Roots, History and Future," available at www.icej.org.

3. For a fuller discussion of how Abraham lives peacefully in the land, see the chapter "Land as Host Country," in Norman C. Habel, *The Land Is Mine: Six Biblical Land Ideologies* (Minneapolis: Fortress, 1995), 115-33.

4. Benny Morris, *Righteous Victims: A History of the Zionist-Arab Conflict, 1881-2001* (New York: Vintage Books, 2001), 164, 171.

5. Baruch Kimmerling, *The Invention and Decline of Israeliness: State, Society, and the Military* (Berkeley: University of California Press, 2001), 113, 127.

Chapter 4

Conquering the Land

By Esther Epp-Tiessen

*When the Lord your God brings you into the land that you are about
to enter and occupy, and he clears away many nations before you—
the Hittites, the Girgashites, the Amorites, the Canaanites, the
Perizzites, the Hivites, and the Jebusites, seven nations mightier and
more numerous than you—and when the Lord your God gives them
over to you and you defeat them, then you must utterly destroy them.
Make no covenant with them and show them no mercy.*
—Deuteronomy 7:1-2

Every year on May 14, Israelis celebrate Independence Day, re-
calling the founding of the state of Israel in 1948 and the realiza-
tion of a dream—the dream of a Jewish homeland reborn. Then
on May 15, Palestinians gather to commemorate the Nakba (Arabic for catastrophe). For them, the anniversary recalls when
many of them, their parents, or grandparents, were expelled
from their homes to make way for the Jewish state. Sadly, an
event that represents salvation for one group represents subjugation for another.

One person who remembered the *Nakba* was Audeh Rantisi.
A boy of eleven in 1948, Rantisi lived with his family in the Pales-
tinian town of al-Lydd (ancient Lydda; today the Israeli city of
Lod). His ancestors had lived in the town for at least 1,600 years.
On a July night, soldiers forced thousands of residents to leave

their homes and to head eastward. Palestinians who resisted or who would not give up their valuables were shot by Israeli troops. Hundreds died of exhaustion and dehydration as they trekked over hills in the scorching mid-summer heat. A memory branded on Rantisi's mind was the image of a young child sucking the breast of her dead mother. Eventually the refugees reached a road where other Palestinians took them by truck to Ramallah. Here they found shelter in what became a refugee camp. Rantisi later recalled,

> Those wretched days and nights in mid-July 1948 continue as a lifelong nightmare because Zionists took away our home of many centuries. For me and a million other Palestinian Arabs, tragedy had marred our lives forever.[1]

Between 750,000 and 900,000 Palestinians, like Rantisi and his family, became refugees in 1948 and 1949. Israel claimed that Arab leaders encouraged people to leave their homes, farms, and businesses and that their departure had been voluntary. In reality, many, like Rantisi, were forced out by threat of death, while the remainder fled to escape the fighting. Most had heard about the village of Deir Yassin, where Israeli forces massacred over 100 Palestinians in April 1948, and they were convinced that the threat was real. With their departure—east to Jordan, south to Egypt, and north to Lebanon and Syria—Israeli forces moved in and razed the villages that Palestinians had tearfully left behind. Within the next few years more than 500 depopulated Palestinian villages were partly or completely destroyed.[2]

Officially, the Israeli government denied any deliberate attempt to rid the new nation of Palestinian Arabs so as to create a predominantly Jewish state. Behind the scenes, however, it promoted the "transfer" of Palestinians out of the land to other Arab nations in the region. Several scholars, including Israelis, have demonstrated how the notion of transfer—a euphemism for expulsion and removal—has from the beginning been deeply embedded within Zionist ideology.[3] It was part of the central task of Zionism—*Kibbush Haadamah*, or "conquest of the land."

As discussed in chapter 3, many Zionists have staked their claim to the land of Palestine on God's promises to Abraham and his descendants. According to some interpretations of Scripture, however, God not only promised the land but also provided divine license to conquer and occupy the land through violence, genocide, and ethnic cleansing. In Deuteronomy 7:1-2, God commands the people of Israel to possess the land by utterly destroying its occupants. The liberation of the people of Israel involves not only exodus but brutal conquest.

The book of Joshua provides the most explicit biblical example of this conquest paradigm. As the book opens, the Israelites are poised to cross the Jordan River and take possession of the Promised Land. The first city they must conquer is Jericho. When they attack Jericho, Joshua tells them, "The city and all that is in it shall be devoted to the Lord for destruction" (6:17). They are not to spare anyone except the prostitute Rahab and her family, because earlier she had assisted the Israelite spies. Every living creature is to be slaughtered. The Israelites comply with God's command: "Then they devoted to destruction by the edge of the sword all in the city, both men and women, young and old, oxen, sheep, and donkeys" (6:21). Scripture reports that "the Lord was with Joshua" (6:27).

The German theologian Ulrike Bechmann has composed a poignant narrative entitled "The Jericho Woman" that imagines the conquest of Jericho from the perspective of those killed by Joshua.

> Hello. You don't know me, but we met already in the story. I'm a woman of Jericho. Not by name—by the way, my name is Nachla.
>
> But I'm in the text, in the last verse you just heard. "men and women, oxen, sheep, and donkeys."
>
> I want to meet you. I'm one of the forgotten ones.
>
> You are going with Joshua?
>
> Well, still the wall of Jericho is there and the gate is open. I'll show you around a bit if you like. You know, we live in a nice city. We have a fountain that never dries up, not even in the summer. This is important, because Jericho is a hot city. Because of the water we have a lot of fruit trees all around the city. And palms! Many of them.
>
> Look at the wall and the big gate. It is well protected. Many travelers and merchants come to our city. We are rich.

If we go down the main street, you can see our temple. It is a fabulous building. And all the silver and gold vessels that are in there! We are really thankful to live in such a good place.

But come to my house. You must be thirsty. I can offer some milk and some fruits. Here is my house.

Look, these are my children. I have three. The daughter is twelve and she is very nice—and she is bright! I want to find a good man for her. Oh, here comes my youngest child. He is three years old. He likes to play around with our donkey. And you know, we sometimes think that the donkey likes him, too.

But, look at the sun, time is running out. You have to hurry to join Joshua again and leave before the gate is closed. Then nobody can go out or in. So, hurry up to go out.

Tomorrow, when the sun rises, the wall will fall down. The city will be burnt. You know, the God of Joshua has no mercy at all, not even for the old ones or the children. Joshua will take all the silver and gold for his God.

So go now, and tomorrow we will meet again—and you will kill me.[4]

Bechmann's narrative dramatically highlights how in the conquest narratives the lives of residents of Jericho and other cities conquered by the invading Israelites are simply erased. The horror of these narratives is difficult to avoid.

After the conquest of Jericho, Joshua leads an attack on Ai. After a first failed attempt because of the sin of one of his men, Joshua succeeds brilliantly. Again, his warriors "utterly destroy" all the inhabitants, as God has commanded, and Joshua has the king of Ai's body hung on a tree. Joshua and the Israelites continue to conquer the kings and peoples of the land of Canaan and to commit other atrocities. Everywhere they go, they inflict "a great slaughter" on the peoples. For each place given into the hand of Israel, the book of Joshua reports that Joshua "struck it with the edge of the sword and every person in it; he left no one remaining" (see variations in 10:28, 30, 31, 34, 37, 38, 40; 11:11, 12, 14). Joshua's actions fulfill God's command (11:15).

The last half of the book of Joshua (chapters 13-24) describes how Joshua divides the land among the twelve tribes and how he encourages them to move in and possess their respective allotments. At the conclusion of the book, Joshua gives his farewell address, reminding the people to remember and be faithful to the God who has driven out the inhabitants of the land before them (24:11-14).

Many Christians and Jews find the book of Joshua offensive in its portrayal of the divinely inspired genocide and ethnic cleansing of the people of Canaan. They prefer to see the Bible as a source of hope, justice, and liberation for oppressed peoples. Certainly many parts of the Bible convey such an ethos. Indeed, numerous liberation movements among the global poor have been inspired by the exodus story of how God rescued and freed an enslaved people. But the book of Joshua demonstrates that alongside the story of deliverance for the people of Israel is the story of conquest and destruction of the Canaanites. The book of Joshua justifies the annihilation of the Canaanites in the name of God. Tragically, God's liberation of one people results in the extermination and oppression of another.

Over the centuries, the conquest paradigm of Joshua has been used to legitimize the oppression, subjugation, and even outright killing of people whose land conquerors want. Throughout history Christian conquerors have been inspired by the stories of biblical conquest to further their own exploits. In the Middle Ages, the Crusaders marched off to Jerusalem to liberate it from "unclean races who polluted and dishonored the Holy Places."[5] In the process they slaughtered Muslims, Jews, and even eastern Christians. Beginning in the fifteenth century, European explorers and missionaries claimed the land of the Americas for God, then killed, enslaved, and dispossessed the indigenous peoples. In the twentieth century, the Boers constructed a theological rationale for apartheid and the subjugation of black South Africans based on the book of Deuteronomy, which portrays the Canaanites in the same way as does the book of Joshua.

Over the past several decades, a growing number of "voices from the margins" have spoken out against readings of the biblical conquest literature that legitimize the conquest paradigm. Some Native Americans, for example, read the story of the exodus and the conquest from the perspective of the Canaanites.[6]

Like the Canaanites, they were already living in the "promised land" when God's "chosen people" moved in. Like the Canaanites, they were killed, displaced, or rounded up onto reserves. Like the Canaanites, they were dispossessed of their land. The exodus-conquest story speaks to them not of liberation but of subjugation. They ask, How can the God of the exodus possibly be a God of deliverance if he is also a God of conquest?

As chapter two introduces, Naim Ateek, a Palestinian Christian theologian and Anglican priest, raises similar questions. Ateek observes that biblical texts of exodus and conquest have been used to justify Israeli displacement and oppression of the Palestinian people. The Palestinian people are like the Canaanites who, if they are not to be slaughtered, are at least to be transferred from the land so the people of Israel (Israelis) may possess it. He points out that, because many Jews and Christians have read the Old Testament as a Zionist text, many Palestinian Christians find it repugnant and have simply stopped reading it.[7]

Ateek demonstrates how the Joshua paradigm has been applied in Israel with respect to the Palestinians. He quotes Israeli religious leader Rabbi Moshe Segal, who compares the Palestinian residents of the West Bank and Gaza to the Amalekites. The Amalekites were the first enemy people that the ancient Israelites encountered upon their escape from Egypt, and God commanded them to "blot out the remembrance of Amalek from under heaven" (Deut. 25:19). Later on, God ordered Saul to "utterly destroy" the Amalekites: "Do not spare them, but kill both man and woman, child and infant, ox and sheep, camel and donkey" (1 Sam. 15: 3). In referring to Palestinians, Rabbi Segal comments, "One should have mercy on all creatures . . . but the treatment of Amalek—is different."[8] Rabbi Israel Hess has written a similar article entitled, "The Genocide Ruling of the Torah [first five books of the Bible]," comparing the Arab people to Amalek and stating that the Torah commands their extermination.[9]

These religious leaders hold a minority view. However, one can argue that their convictions represent an extreme version of a mainstream Israeli tendency to see Palestinian Arabs as second-class at best, with marginal to nonexistent land rights.

In the 1970s, Israeli socio-psychologist Georges R. Tamarin explored the development of prejudice among Israeli youth. In a careful study, he asked students to respond to several verses from the book of Joshua which called for the extermination of people and animals and the destruction of property. He chose Joshua because of its use in the Israeli educational system and its place in shaping Israel's national mythology. From the high percentage of students who approved of Joshua's actions, Tamarin concluded that uncritical use of scriptural texts like those in Joshua "profoundly affects the genesis of prejudices. . . ." Tamarin subsequently lost his position as a professor at Tel Aviv University.[10]

More recently, radical right-wing groups like the Gush Emunim see their mission and mandate as completing the work of Moses and Joshua to "redeem" all the land. Formed in 1974, Gush Emunim has been a major force in the establishment of Jewish settlements within the West Bank. It promotes the creation of these settlements as fulfilling the Torah and hastening the advent of the Messiah and regards the achievement of Greater Israel (annexation of all the land west of the Jordan) as a sacred duty. It considers the Palestinian residents of the land as, at best, "temporary residents" who must be evicted. Though not a political party, Gush Emunim is a major force influencing government policy on settlements. Its settlers have received government support at many levels, not the least being the protection they receive from Israeli soldiers.

The Palestinian city of Hebron in the southern West Bank has been the site of some of the most belligerent settler behavior. In 1979, the wife of Gush Emunim rabbi leader Moshe Levinger led a group of settlers into the heart of the old city. Over the years, the settlers have confiscated homes, businesses, and streets and claimed the land they occupy for God. Their antagonism to Palestinian residents has increased. They routinely spit on, swear at, and assault Palestinians, so that international solidarity and peace groups, such as Christian Peacemaker Teams, have been invited to escort Palestinian children to and from school and in other ways diminish the threat to unarmed and fearful civilians. Many of the 400 or so settlers are heavily armed, even while protected by some 2,000 Israeli soldiers. Settlers related to Gush Emunim have been associated with violent activity against Palestinians in numerous West Bank locations.

Again, it must be said that Gush Emunim and similar groups represent minority views. Many Israelis are deeply dis-

turbed by the attitudes and actions of such settlers. Nevertheless, one must note that Gush Emunim settlements have enjoyed
financial and legal backing from successive Israeli governments.
The majority of Israelis may not share Gush Emunim's vision of
redeeming all of *Eretz Yisrael* (the land of Israel) through settlement, preferring instead to "disengage" from Palestinians by
unilaterally withdrawing from select parts of the Occupied Territories and building walls and fences to contain and limit Palestinians. What both approaches have in common, however, is an
operating assumption that Palestinians do not and should not
have equal rights to and on the land as Israelis.

How should Christians confront the fact that biblical models
of conquest have given rise to religiously motivated conquest
and ethnic cleansing, not only in Palestine-Israel but also elsewhere? What do we do with scriptural passages such as portions
of the book of Joshua which argue that God's people are utterly
to destroy the indigenous inhabitants so that the chosen ones
may possess the land? Somehow Christians need to acknowledge the destructive role these texts have played in history and
find ways to deal with them so that they do not continue to justify the theft of land and crimes against humanity.

There are various ways of dealing with these problematic
texts. One option is to simply disregard parts of the Bible which
provide religious justification for military conquest. As indicated previously, some Palestinian Christians have chosen to do
exactly this—they have simply stopped reading Old Testament
texts which can be used to oppress them. Many other Christians,
who relate more to a God of love and compassion than a God of
violence, have done the same thing. A problem with disregard-
ing the book of Joshua and similar texts is that this approach
does not honestly grapple with the problems posed by the conquest paradigm. If Christians as a whole ignore the Joshua story
and do not critically engage it, some will continue to re-enact it.

Another option is to argue that the Canaanites were sinful
people and therefore deserved to be annihilated. Because they
worshipped other gods, made idols for themselves, and lived
immoral lives, it was necessary for God to exterminate them to
purify the land for the chosen people. This kind of ethical reasoning is extremely dangerous. Humans have an amazing ca-
pacity to demonize their enemies, portraying them as the epit-

ome of evil who must be eliminated at all cost. Time and time again "civilized" Christian people have committed genocide, practiced slavery, and in other ways demeaned "uncivilized" peoples because they saw them as evil. Using the Bible to justify this kind of behavior must stop.

Yet another way of interpreting the conquest paradigm of Joshua is to suggest that the writers of the book were mistaken when they wrote that God commanded the extermination of the Canaanites. Perhaps what these writers heard to be God's command was really their own distorted imaginings. Most ancient societies worshipped tribal gods and sometimes believed that these tribal gods ordered the extermination of enemies. It would not be surprising if the people of Israel, and the writers of Joshua, imagined their God acting in ways similar to the tribal gods of their neighbors. Even though God called the ancient Israelites to be different from the surrounding societies, they often found it difficult to let go of the practices of the cultures which surrounded them.

Perhaps the most helpful hermeneutical key is provided by Naim Ateek. Ateek stresses the importance of theological reflection that brings together biblical truth and the realities of the Palestinian context of oppression. What is the word of God for Palestinians? he asks. The word, says Ateek, is Jesus Christ himself. Christ is the word of God; thus all Scripture must be read through the lens of Christ. Palestinian Christians must interpret any scriptural texts with what they have come to know about the life, death, and resurrection of Jesus.

The key to determining whether a text has authority is whether it agrees with God's revelation through the person of Jesus. Does the text fit with what has been revealed to the community through Jesus Christ? Does it match the character of God that we have come to know through Christ? Does it offer the love, liberation, and justice of Jesus to the community? If so, that passage can be considered to have authority and validity.[11] If not, then Christians must look for ways that the Jesus story re-focuses our understanding of certain texts. So, for example, we can understand Jesus as *Yeshua*, a second Joshua (*Yeshua*) who conquers like Joshua, but in a very different manner.

Ateek demonstrates his hermeneutic specifically with respect to the text describing Joshua's conquest of Jericho and

God's command to devote the city to destruction. He asks, is this passage consistent with how God is revealed in Jesus Christ? No, he concludes. The passage reveals a stage of human understanding of God that is inadequate and incomplete. Christ's incarnation has demonstrated that God is a God of love, justice, and peace whose love, mercy, and compassion extend to all people. The picture of God painted by the writers of Joshua must, for Christians, be read in the light of God's revelation in Jesus, the *Yeshua* who conquers through nonviolent love.

Ateek's hermeneutic provides insight not only for Palestinian Christians but for the wider church. First of all, it grapples with the biblical text from a specific context of oppression that includes dispossession of land, restriction of movement, and military occupation. It reads the conquest paradigm from the perspective of the victimized Canaanites. Most North American Christians, because of their position of power and privilege, have read the conquest narrative from the perspective of the conquerors, the children of Israel. It is critical for us to hear the voice of those from the margins. It is particularly critical for North American Christians to listen to their Palestinian sisters and brothers in the faith.

Second, Ateek's hermeneutic points to Christology—God's revelation made known in Jesus Christ—as the key to interpreting all of Scripture, but particularly those passages which are troublesome. Another way to put it is this: reading the Bible requires Christ-centered discernment. Sometimes biblical texts are in tension with one another. God's Word to Joshua to "utterly destroy" the Canaanites runs counter to Jesus' command to "love your enemies and do good to those who hate you." The task of the Christian community is to discern together how the light of Christ illuminates all other parts of Scripture, transforming our understanding of Israel's history.

Jesus himself recognized that not all portions of the Holy Scriptures reveal God's ultimate will. At one point the Pharisees tested Jesus and asked if it was appropriate for a man to divorce his wife. Jesus responded by asking what Scripture says about the issue. The Pharisees cited Deuteronomy 24:1-4, which states that a man must only supply the proper certificate if he desires to divorce his wife. Jesus responded with an amazing assertion. He declared that the law of Moses on divorce did not reflect the will of God but was a concession to human sinfulness. God's true will was to be found in a different Scripture text, Genesis 2:24, which speaks of God's intention that a man and woman become one flesh, and thereby remain married until death. Jesus recognized that on some issues Scripture contains a diversity of perspectives and that people of faith must search the whole of Scripture to discern the true will of God. In some cases certain biblical texts must take precedence over others.

Jesus' approach to the divorce issue can provide a model for how Christians can approach the book of Joshua. Perhaps the conquest narratives are reflections of ancient culture. Perhaps they speak of how violent human urges are projected onto God. Perhaps they simply represent the incompleteness of human understanding about God's will and way with humanity. Perhaps the conquest narratives can only be received by us as God's Word when read christologically. Jesus' life, death, and resurrection proclaim the way of love, peace, and nonviolence; this is the way God conquers.

The conquest paradigm portrayed in the book of Joshua and related texts has contributed to untold human suffering over the millennia. Much of this suffering has been perpetrated by Christians. Peoples who have understood and appropriated these texts to provide divine sanction for the conquest of others have turned the Bible into an instrument of oppression. It is imperative that Christians today honestly acknowledge and repent of this legacy. Listening to the voices of those victimized by the biblical paradigm of conquest and interpreting the troublesome texts through the revelation of Jesus Christ can help to redeem the Bible and contribute to justice, peace, and healing between peoples.

I began by identifying the contrasting way that Israelis and Palestinians respectively commemorate May 14 and 15—as either liberation or catastrophe (*Nakba*). But numerous Israelis also acknowledge the shadow side of Independence Day and the reality of Nakba. Zochrot is the name of an Israeli group seeking to "remember the Nakba in Hebrew," to build a bridge with Palestinians, and thus to defy the conquest paradigm that plays a role in much Zionist thinking and government policy. Zochrot acknowledges Israeli responsibility for the Nakba and Palestinian pain resulting from it.

As a way of honoring and bringing to remembrance the hundreds of destroyed Palestinian villages, Zochrot posts signs in Hebrew and in Arabic at the sites where these communities once stood. The signs give the names of the former villages and some of their histories. In the words of Zochrot director, Eitan Bronstein, "The catastrophe that occurred to the Palestinians . . . demands some kind of consideration on the part of the historical victors. Simply erecting a sign that tells the story of a demolished village with dignity is recognition of the wrongs committed and the tragedy."[12] In its own way, Zochrot is countering the conquest paradigm and is reaching out to Palestinians in a spirit of reconciliation.

QUESTIONS FOR DISCUSSION

1. Identify situations—past or present—in which Scripture or appeal to God's will has been used to legitimate conquest or other forms of oppression of other peoples.

2. Examine the various ways of interpreting the book of Joshua described above. What are the strengths and or weaknesses of these approaches? What other approaches are you familiar with? Which ones are you drawn to and why?

3. Read 2 Corinthians 3:14-15. Here Paul suggests that Christ removes "the veil" that keeps God's people from understanding God's will and way. How do you respond?

NOTES

1. Audeh G. Rantisi and Ralph K. Beebe, *Blessed are the Peacemakers: A Palestinian Christian in the Occupied West Bank* (Grand Rapids: Zondervan, 1990), 25.

2. For descriptions of these villages, see Walid Khalidi, *All that Remains: The Palestinian Villages Occupied and Depopulated by Israel in 1948* (Washington, D.C.: Institute for Palestine Studies, 1992).

3. See, for example, Nur Masalha, *A Land without People: Israel, Transfer and the Palestinians 1949-1996* (London: Faber and Faber, 1997), as well as Benny Morris, *1948 and After: Israel and the Palestinians* (Oxford: Clarendon Press, 1994).

4. Printed with permission of the author, Ulrike Bechmann.

5. Michael Prior, *The Bible and Colonialism: A Moral Critique* (Sheffield, England: Sheffield Academic Press, 1997), 35.

6. See, for example, Robert Allen Warrior, "A Native American Perspective: Canaanites, Cowboys, and Indians," in R. Sugitharajah, ed., *Voices from the Margin: Interpreting the Bible in the Third World* (Maryknoll, N.Y.: Orbis Books, 1991), 287-95.

7. Naim Stifan Ateek, *Justice and Only Justice: A Palestinian Theology of Liberation* (Maryknoll, N.Y.: Orbis Books, 1989), 77.

8. Quoted in Ateek, 84-85.

9. Ateek, 85.

10. Tamarin's study is described in Prior, *The Bible and Colonialism*, 36-39.

11. Ateek, 79-84.

12. Eitan Bronstein, "Position Paper on Posting signs at the Sites of Demolished Palestinian Villages," www.zochrot.org/index.php?id=343. Accessed on April 27, 2006.

Chapter 5

People Dispossessed of the Land

Esther Epp-Tiessen

They covet fields, and seize them;
 houses, and take them away;
they oppress householder and house,
 people and their inheritance
—Micah 2:2

On October 29, 2005, about 150 Israeli Jews and internally displaced Palestinian citizens of Israel gathered at the site of what was once the Palestinian village of Suhmata, near Israel's border with Lebanon, to remember the past and to look to the future. One of the internally displaced Palestinians, a "son of Suhmata," welcomed former residents and their descendants, concerned Israelis, and international guests, then led them on a walking tour of the village ruins. He pointed out the remains of the school, the mosque, the church, the cemetery, and the gathering place around the village well. He noted where dwellings once stood and where 1,600 people—Muslims and Christians, mostly farmers—had lived together in harmony. He spoke of his longing for the day when the children of Suhmata could return to their home village to live peacefully alongside their Israeli Jewish neighbors.

What happened to Suhmata? On October 28, 1948, Israeli planes bombed the ancient village, killing nineteen people. Wajeeh Sema'n, an eleven-year-old boy at the time, remembers that terrified residents fled to nearby hills to hide. When some snuck back a few days later for food, Israeli soldiers shot them. Thereafter soldiers forbade all Suhmata residents from returning. Consequently, the people of Suhmata dispersed in different directions; today they and their descendants are found around the world. Six hundred remain within Israel's borders. Like Wajeeh, many of them long to return to the place they call their home.

DISPLACEMENT AND DISPOSSESSION

The ruins of Suhmata continue to testify to the story of Palestinian dispossession and displacement—a story repeated throughout Palestine-Israel since the formation of the state of Israel in 1948. As noted in chapter 4, some 750,000 to 900,000 Palestinians lost their homes and their land in the first few years of Israel's existence. The vast majority made their way to refugee camps in neighboring Arab countries and to the areas later known as the West Bank and Gaza. The experience of losing one's home and property marks the experience of the vast majority of Palestinians. Researchers estimate that of a global Palestinian population of 9.7 million, seven million have faced some form of dispossession. Furthermore, two out of five refugees in the world today are Palestinian.[1]

The displacement of people continued over the decades following Israel's founding. Of the 150,000 Palestinians remaining within the borders of the new state, 30,000 had been displaced from their homes. An Israeli law, passed in 1950, considered both refugees and internally displaced persons to be "absentee residents." The new law declared their land the property of the state to be held in perpetuity for exclusive Jewish use. The new Israeli state officially banned former residents from returning to their homes and their land, even those internally displaced Palestinians who had become nominal citizens of the state. Between 1947 and 1949, Israel expropriated about 4.2 million acres (17,178 square km) of Palestinian land.[2]

Between 1949 and 1966, an additional 35,000 to 45,000 Palestinians were displaced. The Six Day War of 1967, when Israel occupied the West Bank, Gaza, East Jerusalem, and the Golan Heights, created 400,000 additional Palestinian refugees, half of whom were displaced for a second time. Since the start of Israel's military occupation, moreover, displacement and dispossession have continued through a variety of means, including land confiscation and expropriation for Israeli settlement construction, house demolitions, and Israeli revocation of Palestinian residency rights.

Along with the displacement of people, dispossession of land also continued after 1949. Between 1949 and 2003 Israel expropriated 1.2 million acres (4,758 square km) of land through a variety of confiscation orders. House demolitions have become numbingly routine. Since 1967, Israel has demolished more than 12,000 Palestinian homes.[3] Some families have witnessed bulldozers level their homes three or four times. Israeli officials usually justify the demolitions by arguing that Palestinian owners do not have permits for home construction. But the reality is that because of discriminatory zoning practices, construction permits are almost impossible for Palestinians to obtain, even when the applicants hold legal title to the land.

Throughout Israel proper and the Occupied Territories, Palestinian land has also been confiscated for the construction of Jewish-only settlements. Since Israel occupied the West Bank, Gaza, and East Jerusalem in 1967, it has constructed housing for about 450,000 Jewish settlers on the land. Nearly half of these homes have been built since 1993. The United Nations has condemned these settlements as illegal because they violate international law. Article 49 of the Fourth Geneva Convention prohibits an occupying state from transferring parts of its own civilian population into the territory it occupies. Nevertheless, the construction of settlements, and the bypass roads needed to link them, has continued at a rapid pace. In summer 2005 the Israeli government withdrew 8,000 Jewish residents from settlements within Gaza because it was becoming too difficult and too costly to defend them, but establishment of new settlements and the enlargement of older ones throughout the West Bank steamed ahead. Geographers estimate that thirty percent of the West Bank is now covered by permanent Jewish settlement blocs.[4]

Israel has also confiscated Palestinian land for its separation barrier. The barrier is a 430 mile (680 km)-long border-like network of construction that, when completed, will isolate Palestinians from Israelis and Palestinians from other Palestinians. In densely populated areas, the barrier consists of massive concrete slabs. In more sparsely populated areas, it is formed by barbed wire, trenches, military roads, and electrified fencing. Critics argue that the barrier, built ostensibly for security purposes (see chapter 8), is yet another way for Israel to solidify its hold on ever larger areas of Palestinian land. At points the wall reaches up to fourteen miles (twenty-three km) into the West Bank to incorporate Jewish settlements geographically into Israel proper.

As of October 2004, Israel had confiscated 8,000 acres (thirty-two square km) of Palestinian land for the construction of the barrier itself, while an additional 89,500 acres (360 square km) were isolated in the region between the Green Line (the armistice line of 1949 dividing Israel from the Occupied Territories) and the barrier.[5] What this means is that Palestinian farmers have been separated from their fields, workers from their jobs, children from their schools, neighbors and even family members from each other.

Israeli-imposed restriction on mobility is yet another form of dispossession for Palestinians. All Palestinians, except for young children with a parent, require Israeli permits to travel beyond their home communities. Residents of the West Bank must have a permit to go to East Jerusalem and even to pass through a checkpoint within the West Bank. Permits are very difficult to obtain—next to impossible for young, single, and unemployed men. Moreover, military officials can "close" the entire West Bank at any time they choose, making the treasured permits useless. For Palestinians, these restrictions on movement are yet another way in which they experience the loss of their land.

THE MEANING OF LAND

As introduced in chapter 1, many Palestinian refugees still possess the keys to the houses and the legal title to the land from which they were expelled. Second- and third-generation refugees continue to identify the village of origin as their home, even though they may never have seen it or been allowed to set foot on its soil. Many families persist in holding out hope for return. Some North Americans may struggle to understand Palestinians' stubborn determination with respect to the right of return. They may wonder why some Palestinians would prefer to remain in overcrowded refugee camps in the West Bank, Gaza, and other Middle Eastern countries, rather than seek a better fortune elsewhere. They may think it more important for Palestinians to look to the future than to focus on the past.

When raising such questions, it is important to understand the meaning of land and home for Palestinians. The land is not simply a piece of real estate that can be bought or sold. Neither is a house simply a dwelling place with walls and a roof that can be easily exchanged for another. Both land and home signify family, inheritance, and identity.[6] Palestinians traditionally lived in agricultural villages their ancestors had inhabited for many generations. Some of them tended olive trees that had been in the family's possession for hundreds of years.

Additionally, extended families lived close to one another, often in the same complex. When a son married, his parents prepared for the wedding by building an additional room or two onto the family home where the new couple would live. Family land holdings and homes were passed on through inheritance to the children. In this way Palestinian identity came to be inseparably linked to a specific piece of land and a specific home.

Elias Chacour, a Melkite (Greek Catholic) priest who is a Palestinian citizen of Israel, describes the relationship between Palestinians and the land this way:

> We belong to the land. We identify with the land, which has been treasured, cultivated, and nurtured by countless generations of ancestors. As a child I joined my family in moving large rocks from the fields. We lay with our backs on the ground and our feet on the rock and pushed, *pushed*, all together. Little by little, "slow by slow," the rock was moved to the side of the field. Perspiration rolled off our bodies, and blood often streamed from our feet, soaking into the ground. It took months to clear the stones from just a small field. The land is so holy, so sacred, to us because we have given it our sweat and blood. . . . Palestinians are at one with their land, and part of them dies when they must be separated from it.[7]

Chacour describes how in the 1950s the Israeli government confiscated the land of Kfar Bir'im, the village his family lived in for hundreds of years. The land was declared to be state land and was annexed to a kibbutz, a Jewish collective farm, located several kilometers away. For Chacour's father, the olive and fig trees were as precious as his own children. Like his ancestors before him, he had cared for them tenderly and lovingly, as he cared for his own sons and daughter. When the orchards were confiscated, he could not bear to be separated from them, so he agreed to work in them as a laborer for the kibbutz. After three years he quit. Chacour explains, "We were becoming slaves, and our personal dignity, our very soul, was too much to sacrifice."[8]

The traditional embroidery of Palestinian women also speaks of the meaning of land and home. The intricate designs and dazzling colors that women choose for their dresses and other tapestries are not simply a matter of individual expression. Rather, these patterns identify a place and a home and, like the olive trees, they are passed on from one generation to another. A woman from Nablus, for example, will wear a different pattern than a woman from Hebron. Her identity and connection to a particular place are clearly visible in her embroidered garment.

For Palestinians, the land—a specific localized piece of land—provides identity. Riad Agbaria laments, "When we lost our land, we lost our mother."[9] Mohammed Othman claims, "The land is part of our heart."[10] Palestinians' deep connection to and identification with the land is what makes dispossession of the land such a profound loss.

NABOTH'S VINEYARD

As chapter 2 introduced, the story of Naboth's vineyard in 1 Kings 21 is a story of the dispossession of land that has close parallels to the Palestinian story. Indeed, Palestinian Christians frequently draw on this biblical account when they reflect theologically on their loss of land. From their perspective, the story of Naboth and his vineyard has been reenacted in Palestine thousands of times since the founding of Israel in 1948.

Naboth was a farmer in the valley of Jezreel in Samaria; his vineyards were on land that had belonged to his family for a long time. King Ahab of Israel had a palace next to the vineyard and desired the land for a vegetable garden. He offered Naboth a good price for the land or a comparable piece of property elsewhere. Naboth refused to part with the land because it was part of his family inheritance. King Ahab went home dejected.

When hearing of what had taken place, Ahab's wife Jezebel challenged him, "Do you now govern Israel?" (v. 7). According to her understanding, kings could take whatever land they desired. She therefore devised a plan for Ahab to take possession of Naboth's vineyard. She sent letters to the elders and nobles of Naboth's home city, ordering them to put Naboth on trial, charge him with cursing God and king, and execute him by stoning. She found two scoundrels to testify against Naboth. The trial proceeded according to Jezebel's plan—Naboth was tried, found guilty, and stoned. Jezebel then reported Naboth's death to King Ahab and urged him to "Go, take possession of the vineyard of Naboth the Jezreelite" (v. 15). Ahab promptly did so.

In the meantime, however, the word of God came to the prophet Elijah, urging him to confront Ahab with the evil of his actions and to say, "Have you killed, and also taken possession?" (v. 19). Elijah went down to Samaria and told Ahab that because Ahab had sold himself to evil by possessing Naboth's vineyard, disaster would come upon him and his household. Both he and Jezebel would be killed and the dogs would lick up their blood from the ground. Elijah's message moved Ahab to repentance; he tore his clothes, put on sackcloth, and fasted. Because Ahab humbled himself, God told Elijah that Ahab would not be killed after all, but there would be consequences in the future.

The parallels between the Naboth story and Palestinian dispossession of land are striking. Naboth himself is much like a traditional Palestinian farmer, caring for vineyards grown on land that has been in his family's possession for a very long time. But more than that, Naboth reflects an understanding of land with which Palestinians identify. When Ahab asks for the land, Naboth refuses because the land is part of his "ancestral inheritance" (v. 3). The land is not something he can readily give away or exchange. The land is a trust to be handed down from generation to generation so families will have economic security (Lev. 25:8-17).

As the caretaker, Naboth is charged with tending the land so he in turn may pass it on to his children, and they to theirs. There is a covenantal understanding of land. In the words of Walter Brueggemann, "Naboth is responsible for the land, but is not in control over it. It is the case not that the land belongs to him but he belongs to the land."[11] As indicated above, this is precisely how many Palestinians relate to their land. For them, as for Naboth, the land represents home, identity, and family extending over the generations. The loss of land for them, if not a literal death like Naboth's, is nevertheless a figurative death.

The second parallel between the Naboth and Palestinian stories is that the land is confiscated by the ruling power of the day. For Naboth, this is the king; for Palestinians, it is the state of Israel. Although King Ahab shows initial reluctance simply to take the land, he is quickly persuaded by the conniving Jezebel that monarchs have the right to possess whatever they desire. Some people say that Jezebel, as a Phoenician, would have had a different understanding of monarchy than Israel; therefore she would have had much less concern about monarchs acting justly toward their subjects than her Israelite husband Ahab. But others note that a royal ideology allowing monarchs to possess whatever land and produce they desire was certainly not limited to non-Israelites.[12] In any case, Ahab's confiscation of Naboth's vineyard is like Israel's confiscation of Palestinian land over the past nearly sixty years.

It is striking that in both the biblical story and the Palestinian story, the confiscation is made to appear legal. Jezebel realizes that taking Naboth's vineyard must have the appearance of due process; therefore, she arranges for Naboth to be tried and charged. The charges and trial are completely phony, but they serve to legitimate Naboth's subsequent stoning and make it seem perfectly legal. Israel's confiscation of Palestinian land is similarly done in ways that conform to Israeli law (and thus have the appearance of legality) but frequently defy international understandings of law and human rights. As indicated previously, in the wake of 1948, Israel determined that Palestinians had abandoned their homes and were "absentee residents"—even though most had been forced out and desperately wished to return. Any land deemed belonging to absentees could be legally confiscated. This process has continued.

Additionally, Israel demolishes Palestinian homes because their owners do not have building permits, even though Israeli officials make it virtually impossible to obtain these permits. Israel confiscates land from Palestinians in the Occupied Territories on the basis of Ottoman-era laws designed to help the state promote public use of land and make land available to landless peasants, then uses the confiscated land to construct settlements for exclusive Jewish use. Moreover, Israel's ideology of national security has allowed for the creation of a whole system of military orders in the Occupied Territories—relating to the uprooting of trees, the control of water, and the restriction of movement—all of which add up to a legal system that tightly circumscribes Palestinian life and contributes to Palestinian dispossession. Israel, like Jezebel, misuses the law to give the appearance of legality and legitimacy to the confiscation of Palestinian land.

The story from 1 Kings 21 places Naboth's vineyard in the Jezreel Valley. In biblical times, as today, the Jezreel Valley was prized for its fertile and well-watered soil. One can imagine that Naboth's vineyard bore abundant fruit, providing a good living for Naboth and his family. Perhaps this is precisely why Ahab desired the vineyard—he knew the land was productive and water readily available. It is no accident that as Israel confiscates Palestinian land it also seeks out the best land with the most abundant water sources. The Jordan River Valley on the West Bank, like the Jezreel Valley, is very fertile and, with irrigation, extremely productive. This prized valley, though part of the Occupied Territories, is now controlled by Israel, with most of it given to agricultural settlements: Israeli military orders prevent almost all Palestinians from going to the valley. In the Qalqilya region in the West Bank, the separation barrier has been constructed in such a way as to give Israel complete control of the most plentiful water aquifer in the entire West Bank.

The hopeful dimension of the Naboth story, from the Palestinian as well as the larger Christian perspective, is God's response. Ahab's and Jezebel's actions toward Naboth provoke God to anger. God regards the killing of Naboth and the possession of his land as grievous sins which must be addressed. Thus God commands Elijah to confront Ahab and to describe the punishment that awaits him and Jezebel. God is thus revealed as a God with a profound concern for justice and a God who will stand up for victims of injustice. God will not allow the dispossession and the injustice to go unanswered, even if perpetrated by powerful rulers. God will hear the cry of the dispossessed and vindicate their cause. God will also show mercy when perpetrators of injustice turn from their evil ways. For Palestinians the story offers the hope of liberation.

The land of Palestine is inscribed on the heart of the Palestinian soul. Therefore the loss of land is like a wound that does not heal. Rather, the pain of this wound is taken up by succeeding generations, some of whom may have never set foot on the land of their ancestors, but who nonetheless name it as their home. Palestinians identify with the specific pieces of land that belonged to their families as well as the land of their people as a whole. They long for a day when they live with justice on their land and in their land.

QUESTIONS FOR DISCUSSION

1. Compare the different understandings of land reflected in the story of Naboth's vineyard. Which understanding is closest to your own? What are the factors that influence your understanding?

2. Is there a refugee story or story of dispossession within your family circle? What is the meaning of that story for family members? Does the story or its significance change over time?

3. What are other contemporary parallels to the story of Naboth's vineyard? Can you see God at work in these situations? How might the story of Naboth's vineyard and the Palestinian context relate to the story of dispossession of native (aboriginal) persons in North America? How might God's justice be served?

SUGGESTIONS FOR ACTION

1. Volunteer with groups in your community that offer support to refugees.

2. Pray for refugees worldwide to find secure dwellings.

NOTES

1. All statistics are from *Survey of Palestinian Refugees and Internally Displaced Persons, 2003* (Bethlehem: Badil Resource Center for Palestin-

ian Residency and Refugee Rights, 2004).

2. *Survey of Palestinian Refugees and Internally Displaced Persons, 2003.*

3. Jeff Halper, *Obstacles to Peace: A Re-Framing of the Palestinian-Israeli Conflict,* 3rd. ed. (Jerusalem: Israeli Committee Against Home Demolitions, 2005), 17.

4. *Israeli Committee Against Home Demolitions.*

5. *Al Majdal* 26 (Summer 2005), 3-4

6. See Audeh G. Rantisi and Ralph K. Beebe, *Blessed are the Peacemakers: A Palestinian Christian in the Occupied West Bank* (Grand Rapids: Zondervan, 1990), 87.

7. Elias Chacour with Mary E. Jensen, *We Belong to the Land: The Story of a Palestinian Israeli who lives for Peace and Reconciliation* (San Francisco: Harper San Francisco, 1990), 80.

8. Chacour, 79.

9. Comment made by Dr. Riad Agbaria at the Intercultural Conference on Land, Peoples and Identities, Bethlehem, November 6-12, 2005.

10. Author's interview with Mohammed Othman of Jayyous, November 9, 2005.

11. Walter Brueggemann, *The Land* (Philadelphia: Fortress Press, 1977), 93.

12. See Norman C. Habel, *The Land is Mine: Six Biblical Land Ideologies* (Philadelphia: Fortress Press, 1995), 30-31.

Chapter 6

Living Justly in the Land

By Christi Hoover Seidel

You shall not wrong or oppress a resident alien, for you were aliens in the land of Egypt. You shall not abuse any widow or orphan. If you do abuse them, when they cry out to me, I will surely heed their cry; my wrath will burn, and I will kill you with the sword, and your wives shall become widows and your children orphans.
—Exodus 22:21-24

On 26 August 2003, Rula Ashtiya was forced to give birth on the ground, on a dirt road by the Beit Furik checkpoint after Israeli soldiers refused her passage. Her baby died a few minutes later. She was deeply traumatized, and when Amnesty International visited her several weeks later she could hardly bring herself to talk about her ordeal. Twenty-nine-year-old Rula went into labor in her eighth month of pregnancy, in the early morning. Her husband Daoud called the ambulance and was told that he and Rula should go to the Beit Furik checkpoint, between their village and the [West Bank] town of Nablus, because the ambulance could not get past the checkpoint and would wait for them on the other side. Rula and Daoud set out for the checkpoint a few minutes from their village, Salem. It was already light and given Rula's obvious condition they did not expect problems crossing the checkpoint. However, the Israeli soldiers refused them passage.
—From a 2005 Amnesty International Report[1]

THE MARGINALIZED

Rula and Daoud's story, unfortunately, is not unique. Several other infants have died during or after childbirth at Israeli checkpoints inside the occupied West Bank, because mothers in labor were not allowed to pass through to get to hospitals. Children are particularly vulnerable in situations of conflict. Children almost always bear the brunt of injustice and violence, be it inequities in schooling, lack of proper health care, poor nutrition, or the absence of one or both parents to raise and protect them to the best of their ability. Sadly, the Palestinian-Israeli conflict is no different. Since September 2000, hundreds of Palestinian and Israeli children have lost their lives in the course of the conflict.[2] Schooling for Palestinian children has been routinely disrupted due to curfews and checkpoints, and children's health and nutrition have suffered as Palestinian poverty and unemployment have grown.

Throughout Scripture God is portrayed as possessing special concern for the poor, the weak, and the vulnerable. Widows and orphans, sojourners and aliens, are singled out as those vulnerable groups that God hears and defends. In ancient Israel resident aliens were those who fell outside of an established community or family group and thus had less personal security than others. God's concern in Exodus for the widow and the resident alien demonstrates God's passionate care for those whose voices are routinely silenced and marginalized because their vulnerable position in society renders them more susceptible to injustice and violence at the hands of the powerful. God reminds the people not to oppress aliens or abuse widows and orphans, for they were once aliens as well.

The pressing question in Exodus appears to be, "Who has the power?" God's command to act justly to the aliens in the land suggests that Israel possessed a degree of power, power not to be used unjustly. God draws a clear parallel between the Israelites' new position and that of their former Egyptian slave-masters, making it clear that they are not above these standards of conduct when it comes to power, because if the tables are turned, they could be the ones suffering.

Today, the modern state of Israel wields substantial power. It boasts one of the world's most advanced militaries, a relatively strong economy, and close political and economic ties with the

United States. How will Israel use this power? To build defensive fortifications and offensive walls? To dispossess farmers of their land? Or will it perhaps open itself to the cries of those marginalized by policies of military occupation, remembering that God's people are called to practice justice?

THE COMMAND TO LIVE JUSTLY

How are God's people to live justly in the land? To answer this question we must first articulate an understanding of justice. Palestinian Anglican priest Naim Ateek describes justice as

> a quality that a person should possess—being righteous and fair. It is also a relationship that a person must maintain—not gaining advantage by taking what belongs to others. Each dimension is important; each can be seen as a natural extension of the other. The inner quality produces the outer relational aspect of a just living with other people."[3]

Exclusivist land policies and practices clearly do not conform to this understanding of justice. Greed coupled with a focus on one's perceived needs above the needs of others often drives unjust land practices in the Occupied Territories. The separation barrier, Israeli-only settlements built on confiscated Palestinian land, road networks off-limits to Palestinians, roadblocks, and checkpoints all form what Israeli anthropologist Jeff Halper calls a matrix of control through which Palestinians lose access to land. This matrix of control obstructs and prevents Palestinian movement to schools, hospitals, work, and family. The matrix functions as a form of structural violence that defines daily life for average Palestinians.

Direct forms of violence supplement and reinforce these structures of violence and dispossession. For example, Israeli settlers from Ma'on, in the Hebron hills of the southern West Bank, have persistently harassed Palestinian school children from several villages who must walk past the settlement to go to their school in Tuwani village. International volunteers who have accompanied these children on their walk to school have been beaten by these settlers, leading to hospitalization. The message to the villagers is clear: The land belongs to us and we will do what we must to possess and rule it.

If, as Ateek rightly observes, there is an "inner quality" of justice, one of opening oneself to equality with others, there is also an inner quality of injustice and violence, the quality of dehumanizing the other. One could argue, for example, that many Zionists before 1948 (and later many Israelis) viewed the indigenous Palestinian Arabs not as people to engage but as obstacles to the Zionist vision of an exclusively Jewish state. David Ben-Gurion, one of the Zionist leaders before 1948 and Israel's first prime minister, wrote in 1948 that "it is clear that England belongs to the English, Egypt to the Egyptians, and Judea to the Jews. In our country there is room only for Jews. We will say to the Arabs: 'Move over'; if they are not in agreement, if they resist, we will push them by force."[4] Moreover, violence, be it carried out by a state's military or by armed insurgents, dehumanizes its victims in many ways, turning victims of war into "collateral damage" and blurring civilian/soldier distinctions.

JUSTICE EMPOWERED
THROUGH CHRIST'S LOVE

In Exodus, God clearly warns those in power that they are not to take advantage of the marginalized members of their society. "You shall not pervert the justice due to your poor in their lawsuits," God cautions (Exod. 23:6). Practicing injustice against others will have consequences—although it is clear from the passage with which we began that vengeance is a matter for God, not for people to take into their own hands.

In the New Testament we see how God ultimately responds to human acts of sin, violence, and injustice—by sending his only son to embody perfect justice and peace and to defeat the powers of sin. To understand justice correctly, we must allow our understandings of justice to be molded by Jesus' life, death, and resurrection. We must possess the love of Christ highlighted by the confession, "For God so loved the world" (John 3:16). Here we learn most clearly what living justly means—God's love encompasses all of the world, all of creation, and so we dare not judge, oppress, or ostracize persons or groups based on ethnicity, religion, class-structures, or gender. God's action in Jesus is one of building bridges that connect, of networks that embrace, rather than of establishing walls that exclude.

Audeh Rantisi, a Palestinian Anglican priest who was also a refugee, cites John's proclamation of the wideness of God's love as a pivotal text in the development of his vision for a just peace in the land for Palestinians and Israelis:

> "For God so loved the world that he gave his only begotten son, that whosoever. . . ." Whosoever! That meant not only me, but the rest of the world! . . . This conversion experience did not decrease my passion for a national homeland. In some ways acceptance of God's teaching increased my concern for justice and sharpened my Palestinian nationalism. It helped me know that while hating what the Zionists did, I could love them as human beings. . . . The paradox is fascinating: The spiritual experience heightened my disgust for injustice but increased my understanding of its causes and my empathy for its perpetrators. All of us are capable of inflicting terrible indignities; all of us can find forgiveness and redemption in the power of God's love.[5]

Rantisi was empowered by God to see his oppressor as a human being. This empowerment by God to forgive those who made him a refugee triumphs over cycles of violence and retribution. Such forgiveness, as Rantisi observed, does not diminish a passion for doing justice in the land but instead places justice within a framework of reconciliation. Justice for Palestinians, then, is not about retribution against Israelis; rather, it is about establishing right relations between Israelis and Palestinians.

JUSTICE THROUGH INTERNATIONAL LAW

As a powerful nation, Israel today uses its military might to shore up its control over all of historical Palestine, all in the name of security. Yet, for all of the land gained by the Israeli government, Israel's integrity and true security are being compromised. For all of the checkpoints and walls Israel erects in the Occupied Territories, Israelis ironically find themselves in prisons of their own making. No matter how extensive Israel's matrix of control over Palestinian lives becomes, fear for average Israelis is not far behind. Israelis, not only Palestinians, are hemmed in by Israel's practices of dispossession. To call on Israel to practice justice, then, is not only in the interests of Palestinians; it is for the good of Israelis.

How, then, can the state of Israel act in justice? As a starting point, Israel, like other nations of the earth, should comply with international law. With regard to its treatment of Palestinian refugees, its determination to maintain control over the Occupied Territories, and its construction of civilian settlements in those Occupied Territories, however, Israel acts against international law and resolutions. In 1949, The UN passed General Assembly Resolution 194, calling for the return of and compensation for refugees from the 1948 war willing to live in peace. It also stated that the refugees should regain their homes and property as early as possible. The UN resolution meshed well with existing international humanitarian law regarding refugees. Israel in fact affirmed UNGA 194 to obtain membership in the United Nations. To this day, however, Israel has refused to allow any refugees to return to their homes.[6]

On November 22, 1967, the United Nations passed Security Council Resolution 242, calling on Israel to withdraw from the territories it occupied during the 1967 war. Though this resolution served as the basis for Israel's peace agreements with Egypt and Jordan, Israel, opposing the international community, continues to argue that it doesn't apply to all of the Occupied Territories. Israel therefore refuses to consider a full withdrawal from East Jerusalem, the West Bank, and the Gaza Strip.

The Fourth Geneva Convention, published and put into force in 1950, relates to the protection of civilians during times of war by the enemy or the occupying foreign power.[7] While responsible under the Geneva Conventions for the protection and well-being of Palestinian civilians in the Occupied Territories, Israel implements policies that harm the well-being of Palestinian civilians: The case of Rula and Daoud told at the beginning of this chapter is but one of thousands of examples of ways in which Palestinian civilian life has been disrupted and damaged by Israeli practices.

Palestinian Christians like Audeh Rantisi and Naim Ateek suggest that for Israel to have true security, it must practice justice by abiding by international resolutions and by living up to its obligations under international law for how it operates in the Occupied Territories. While Israel continues to ignore the call of justice, Christians worldwide should join Palestinian Christians in calling Israel to live up to God's call in Exodus to practice justice in the land, to heed the voices of the marginalized, to use its power to build bridges of reconciliation for the mutual well-being of all in the land rather than walls of dispossession and control.

ISRAELIS RESPONDING
TO THE CALL FOR JUSTICE

Many Israelis lament that their government fails to do justice in the land; they respond by fervently striving for changes in Israeli practices and policies. One Israeli rabbi who takes the biblical call to justice seriously is Rabbi Arik Ascherman, a member of the group Rabbis for Human Rights. Ascherman works tirelessly for justice for all people in the land, often joining Palestinians in nonviolent demonstrations against house demolitions, the uprooting of trees, and the building of the separation barrier.

Ascherman, one should note, considers himself a Zionist, in the sense that he reads Scripture as promising the land to the Jewish people. He is quick to add that he also believes that people and human life are more important than the land and that God's promise of the land can be withdrawn depending on how the Jewish people act in the land. Israeli practices of house demolition, the uprooting of farmers' trees on the pretext of "security," and the construction of Israeli-only settlements and the separation barrier as ways to solidify control over land are examples of how Israel fails to practice justice in the land.

Ascherman recognizes that Palestinians have legitimate claims to the land. Palestinian and Jewish claims to the land, he believes, can be realized either in a single, binational state or in two separate states, living side-by-side. At a recent workshop including Palestinians, Israelis, and expatriates, a questioner asked Palestinians in the room whether or not they could accept Ascherman's conviction that God had promised the land to the Jewish people, given that his moral and ethical convictions lead him to work for human rights. One Palestinian replied, "We have to come to reality and therefore we can live together side by side, with equality, understanding, working together and in accordance with international law and the 1967 borders." A second Palestinian added that "Our struggle is against occupation and humiliation, not against the Jewish religion itself." This led a third Palestinian to explain, "We are struggling together. We see him as a person who supports us. Our kids ask us the difference between him and the soldier. Our religions are our religions."

The reaction of the workshop participants to Ascherman's input underscored the vitality and importance of persons of faith, be they Jewish, Christian, or Muslim, working for justice in the land. As Christians, we can pray that the numbers of Palestinians and Israelis joining people like Rabbi Ascherman in the hard work of doing justice might increase.

QUESTIONS FOR DISCUSSION

1. What are some examples of the abuse of power in the Old Testament? In current events?

2. Palestinian Christians Naim Ateek and Audeh Rantisi both consider justice to be intertwined with love, peace, and mercy. How is this interconnection seen in the person of Jesus?

3. Power mixed with greed often leads to oppression. How can the power we possess as Christians in affluent Western societies be used for justice, peace, and reconciliation in Palestine-Israel?

4. How does Ascherman's vision for justice and human rights conflict with the ideology of the Zionist fathers of the modern state of Israel such as Ben-Gurion?

SUGGESTION FOR ACTION

1. Show MCC's *The Dividing Wall* DVD/video to your Sunday school class or small group (see www.mcc.org).

2. Contact MCC's offices in Washington, D.C., and Winnipeg, Canada, for suggestions about how you can contact elected officials regarding justice and peace in Palestine-Israel.

3. Pray for deliverance from evil as an acknowledgement that power has the potential for oppression as well as for good. Ask for God's guidance on using power and resources for the good of humankind.

NOTES

1. "Israel and the Occupied Territories: Conflict, Occupation and Pa-

triarchy—Women Carry the Burden" (web.amnesty.org/library/index/engmde150162005). Updated on 31 March 2005.

2. See www.rememberthesechildren.org/remember2006.html

3. Naim Stifan Ateek, *Justice and Only Justice: A Palestinian Theology of Liberation* (Maryknoll, N.Y.: Orbis Books, 1989), 116.

4. Colin Chapman, *Whose Promised Land?* (Batovia, Ill.: Lion Publishing, 1992), 51.

5. Audeh Rantisi, *Blessed are the Peacemakers: The Story of a Palestinian Christian* (Grand Rapids: Zondervan, 1990), 48.

6. Sonia K. Weaver, *What is Palestine-Israel? Answers to Common Questions* (Scottdale, Pa.: Herald Press, 2007), 24-26.

7. See en.wikipedia.org/wiki/Fourth_Geneva_Convention.

Chapter 7

Caring for the Land

Christi Hoover Seidel

You shall observe my statutes and faithfully keep my ordinances, so that you may live on the land securely. The land will yield its fruit, and you will eat your fill and live on it securely. Should you ask, What shall we eat in the seventh year, if we may not sow or gather in our crop? I will order my blessing for you in the sixth year, so that it will yield a crop for three years. When you sow in the eighth year, you will be eating from the old crop; until the ninth year, when its produce comes in, you shall eat the old. The land shall not be sold in perpetuity, for the land is mine; with me you are but aliens and tenants.
—Leviticus 25:18-23

The land, the book of Leviticus insists, ultimately belongs to God. To the extent that land is ours, it is ours on a temporary basis. The land, in a very real sense, is on loan to us from God, who has entrusted humanity with the care and tending of the earth and its resources. Land and other natural resources should not be exploited; instead, every seventh year, the land should be given a rest (see also Lev. 25:2-5). Care of the land in Leviticus is also bound up with security—the security of being able to sustain the land's productivity and fertility over long periods of time, and thus of having enough to eat. What must God's people do to live securely in the land? They must obey God's laws and regulations and care for land. Such a concept of security differs dramatically from approaches to security based on military strategies and fortified borders.

SUSTAINABILITY AND SECURITY

Saleh Qademi is a Palestinian farmer, born and raised in the northern West Bank town of Jayyous. Like his ancestors before him, Saleh farms for a living, growing olives, guava, eggplant, tomatoes, sweet peppers, and cucumbers. The town of Jayyous has 3,250 acres (ca. thirteen square km) of farmland, but now 2,250 of those acres (ca. nine square km), including all of Saleh's fields, fall on the western side of the separation barrier Israel constructed next to Jayyous from 2002 to 2004. Almost all of the Jayyous' wells tapping into the West Bank's most plentiful aquifer also fall on the western side of the wall. Residents of Jayyous note that many in Israel have started talking about the separation barrier as the future border of the state of Israel. They worry what these developments mean about future access to their fields and water sources. This concern has intensified following Israeli confiscation of some of the land west of the barrier, confiscations Jayyous residents assume will lead to the expansion of the Israeli settlement west of Jayyous.

Since the construction of the separation barrier, Saleh has had to obtain a permit from the Israeli military government in the Occupied Territories to reach his fields. For many months Saleh, along with most farmers in Jayyous, could not obtain a permit. Now he has one, but having a permit in hand does not always guarantee access to his land. The Israeli soldiers do not always open the gates in the barrier, and when they do, it is only for certain periods in the day—at most an hour in the morning, an hour at noon, and an hour in the evening, but often much less. Gone are the days when Saleh and his family could rise before dawn and get an early start to the harvest or the planting. Gone are the days when Saleh could stay on his land until late in the evening to work and enjoy tea under his trees and the open sky with his neighbors and friends.

Saleh loves the freedom of being an independent farmer and is soberly realistic about the chances of finding other employment given the high unemployment rates in the Occupied Territories. He fears for the future of the land and his children. He can't even think about selling the land because of his strong connection to it. "It would be like selling ourselves," he shares. "If I leave the land and travel, I always miss it. I wonder how the land is doing, and we feel the land misses us."[1] Care for the land and inclusive security on the land go hand-in-hand. Farmers like Saleh tend to the land as they would care for a loved one, and yearn for secure existence on that land.

CREATION AND CONFLICT

When one's concern about land, however, is how to dominate and control it, care and nurture for the land too often fall out of view. The Israeli government's concern to develop and maintain demographic and military control over historical Palestine, from the Jordan River to the Mediterranean Sea, leads to the construction of walls, fences, and road networks. These barriers, Israeli and Palestinian environmentalists stress, create serious ecological damage. For Christian Zionists, meanwhile, the land is little more than a stage on which the events of Armageddon are to unfold. If the planet has no future, if one expects the imminent destruction of all earthly existence, not surprisingly concern for the environment falls low on the list of priorities. Land is too often seen as an object to be used in a battle for domination and control, rather than as a gift entrusted to humanity for nurture and for sharing with others.

Those who drive through the Occupied Territories today can easily see in the landscape effects of the conflict. Israeli bulldozers have uprooted thousands of trees in recent years to make way for the separation barrier, most of which lies in the Occupied Territories, cutting Palestinian villages off from much of their farmland. Meanwhile, some of the last remaining forested mountaintops in the West Bank have been confiscated and cleared to build settlements. People who came from Jerusalem to Bethlehem about ten years ago remember the green forest area just off of the main road toward Hebron on the hill known by Palestinians as Jebel Abu Ghneim. Most of the land on this hill is owned by Palestinian Christians from Beit Sahour, east of Bethlehem.

Now a large settlement, Har Homa, looms where the trees once stood, with cranes expanding the settlement down the mountainside. The Israeli government offers financial incentives and tax breaks to its Jewish citizens who will come and fill the housing developments in these settlements. In many cases, some of the housing within expanding settlements remains empty, yet the construction continues.

A desire to control the water resources in the Occupied Territories drives much Israeli land confiscation. Specifically, Israel has access to eighty-five percent of the West Bank's ground water resources, leaving Palestinians with only fifteen percent.[2] The Fourth Geneva Convention prohibits occupying powers such as Israel from expropriating natural resources in the Occupied Territories. As with other portions of the Geneva Conventions, Israel simply disregards this prohibition. Water experts note, meanwhile, that Israel's separation barrier in the Occupied Territories solidifies Israeli control over the West Bank water resources. Furthermore, Israel has also cut off the Jordan Valley from the rest of the West Bank, ensuring Israeli control over the Valley's vital water resources.

Even as Israel's occupation policies and practices wreak environmental havoc inside the Occupied Territories, Israel disingenuously appeals to environmental concerns to limit Palestinian construction. The Jerusalem municipality, for example, routinely designates open areas in Palestinian neighborhoods of East Jerusalem as "green areas" off limits to building as a way to limit Palestinian growth. On more than one occasion, however, "green areas" in which Palestinians might have been able to build have later been rezoned to allow for Israeli construction. In the Negev (in Arabic, *Naqab*) desert in southern Israel, meanwhile, the so-called "Green Patrol" regularly attacks and harasses Palestinian Bedouin communities, destroying fields and confiscating livestock. Severe restrictions on the development of Palestinian Bedouin communities are thus presented as "green" concerns about the Negev's environment.

The greening of the landscape can also sometimes be used to erase the past. Before 1967, in the westernmost part of the West Bank, lay three Palestinian villages: Imwas (associated with the biblical Emmaus), Yalu, and Beit Nuba. During the Six Day War of 1967 the Israeli military forced the villagers out by gunpoint, then razed the towns. Villagers from Imwas, Yalu, and Beit Nuba now live in Ramallah and other parts of the West Bank. The Jewish National Fund, with donations from Jewish communities in Canada, planted a forest on the site of the destroyed villages, a site that later came to be known as Canada Park. Many Israelis visit the park, picnic there, and enjoy the natural setting—without knowing the tragic history of the place.[3]

CREATION AND PEACE

In days to come the mountain of the Lord's house shall be established as the highest of the mountains, and shall be raised up above the hills. Peoples shall stream to it, and many nations shall come and say: "Come, let us go up to the mountain of the Lord, to the house of the God of Jacob; that he may teach us his ways and that we may walk in his paths." For out of Zion shall go forth instruction, and the word of the Lord from Jerusalem. He shall judge between many peoples, and shall arbitrate between strong nations far away; they shall beat their swords into plowshares, and their spears into pruning hooks; nation shall not lift up sword against nation, neither shall they learn war any more; but they shall all sit under their own vines and under their own fig trees, and no one shall make them afraid; for the mouth of the Lord of hosts has spoken. (Mic. 4:1-4)

The prophet Micah shows us that true security and care for the land stand in contradiction to the ways of learning and carrying out warfare. God's will is that weapons be turned into tools for the cultivation and care of the land. Furthermore, Micah links this renunciation of violence in favor of care for the land to a future of landed security in which all will have a portion of land, a safe space with vines and trees under which they might sit and whose fruit they might eat. Today, neither Palestinian nor Israeli live secure under vine and fig tree, and the weapons of war have yet to be turned to plowshares and pruning hooks. Israelis and Palestinians both fear physical violence, while farmers like Saleh are isolated from the land they care for.

Michael Crosby, in reflections on the Lord's Prayer, connects God's will for the earth to our responsibilities not only toward natural resources but also toward another part of creation—fellow humans. "The resources of the earth are for everyone," Crosby writes. "To use one's power to deny others access to those resources is to make oneself a god—for only God can use power in such a way as to deny other humans access to the earth's resources. To do otherwise is to assume divine power over other human beings. This applies equally to individuals, interpersonal groupings, and infrastructures (including nations)."[4]

In Matthew 5:5, Jesus declares, "Blessed are the meek, for they will inherit the earth." What earth are they to inherit if the land is not properly tended? What kind of inheritance is this for them? Is it surprising that those who are gentle and lowly in heart are called to be the ones entrusted with the earth? Throughout the Gospels, Jesus constantly compares the kingdom of heaven to the bounty of the land: The kingdom is like mustard seeds, wheat and weeds, yeast, a field with a hidden treasure, and scattered seeds.

Creation, like humankind, is vulnerable. The relationship between creation and humanity is symbiotic, with the care of one depending on the care of the other. The earth does not suffer alone when it is not cared for. Rather, every living creature in the creation is affected and afflicted by the violations of the earth.

Palestinians whose olive groves, citrus orchards, and tomato and cucumber fields have not been damaged and destroyed by bulldozers and tanks often say that each tree, each acre of the field, is as dear to them as their children. The trees represent their long family histories and a secure source of income plus provide olives and oil for the table. They give shade in the hot summer sun and a place to sit and drink coffee with friends and neighbors. The trees provide a place for their children to play. The trees, in short, embody Palestinian rootedness to the land.

Trees are vulnerable and life-giving. It should be no surprise, then, that the olive branch has for centuries been a symbol of peace. For those who work the land, the earth and its bounty cannot be separated from the promise of peace. For Palestinians, the olive tree's branch is not only a symbol of peace—the olive tree itself is a symbol of what Palestinians call *sumud*, a steadfast commitment to remaining rooted on the land.

For Mitri Raheb, the Palestinian pastor of the Lutheran parish in Bethlehem, caring for olive trees is a concrete way of embodying the Christian hope in God's kingdom of peace and reconciliation. "Holding to a hopeful vision in the context of war gives hope a new meaning," Raheb observes. "It is no longer something we see but rather something we practice, something we live, something we advocate, something we plant. At times when we feel as if the world must be coming to an end tomorrow, our call is not to wait, not to cry, nor to surrender," Raheb notes. Rather, he insists, echoing Martin Luther's counsel about what he would do if he knew the world would end tomorrow, "our only hopeful vision is to go out today into our garden, into our society, and plant olive trees. If we don't plant any trees today, there will be nothing tomorrow. But if we plant a tree today, there will be shade for the children to play in, there will be oil to heal the wounds, and there will be olive branches to wave when peace arrives."[5]

DISCUSSION QUESTIONS

1. What connections do you see between peace and care for the environment?

2. What are some ideologies of control in North America that have adverse environmental effects?

3. In addition to Leviticus and Micah, what parts of Scripture do you see as speaking to the connections between peace and care for the land?

SUGGESTIONS FOR ACTION

1. Visit the website of the Applied Research Institute-Jerusalem (ARIJ) (www.arij.org) to learn more about the impact of military occupation on the land and water resources in the West Bank. MCC works with ARIJ on water harvesting and recycling projects in the southern West Bank.

2. MCC supports the YMCA's Women's Training Program, which, in addition to giving women business and small-livestock-management skills and small loans from a revolving loan fund, works with Palestinian women to reduce waste and to recycle at the household level. To learn more about the East Jerusalem YMCA's work, visit www.ej-ymca.org/site.

3. Pray that we might relate to creation with humility. Pray for the earth and all of the living creatures upon it to experience renewal, even in the face of human conflict and greed. Pray for peace upon the earth and its inhabitants.

NOTES

1. Ed Nyce, "First Person: Saleh Qademi," *A Common Place* (September/October 2004), 14.

2. Detailed discussion of the control of water resources in the Occupied Territories can be found in the study, *Water in Palestine—Scarcity, Instability, and Conflict* (Bethlehem: Applied Research Institute-Jerusalem, 2004). Available at www.arij.org.

3. For more information on these three villages and Canada Park, visit the Zochrot Association website: www.zochrot.org.

4. Michael H. Crosby, *Thy Will Be Done: Praying the Our Father as Subversive Activity* (Maryknoll, N.Y.: Orbis Books, 1977), 31.

5. Mitri Raheb, *Bethlehem Besieged: Stories of Hope in Times of Trouble* (Minneapolis: Fortress Press, 2004), 157.

Chapter 8

Security in the Land

Esther Epp-Tiessen

If your enemies are hungry, give them bread to eat;
and if they are thirsty, give them water to drink. . . .
—Proverbs 25:21

Robi Damelin is an Israeli Jewish mother. On March 3, 2002, her life was shattered. Her youngest son, David, a gifted musician and talented educator, was shot and killed by a Palestinian sniper. Elham Elshoabe, a Palestinian mother, suffered a similar devastating loss only a few months later. On September 1, 2002, Israeli tanks rolled into her family's hometown of Nablus on the West Bank. Her twenty-seven-year-old son Ghasan ran into the street to warn a group of children and to urge them to go home. Ghasan was shot by Israeli soldiers and died a week later.

THE IMPASSE OF INSECURITY
The stories of these two mothers and their sons epitomize the tragedy of the Israeli-Palestinian conflict—the loss of precious human life. David and Ghasan are only two of the thousands of victims of the ongoing conflict. While most deaths have occurred during periods of full-fledged war, the death toll continues to rise on a daily basis. Between September 2000, when the second intifada (or uprising) began, and November 2005,

more than 1,000 Israelis and 3,500 Palestinians were killed. Of
the Israelis killed, 138 were minors under the age of eighteen. Of
the Palestinians killed, 669 were minors.[1] Each death leaves in its
wake a grieving family and a shaken community.

But death is not the only tragedy resulting from this protracted conflict. During the same period, thousands more persons, mostly Palestinian, were injured by live ammunition, rub-
ber bullets, tear gas, and beatings. Many of the injured sustained
permanent disabilities. Even larger numbers suffered psychological trauma as a result of personally experiencing or witness-
ing acts of political violence. Many Palestinian children, nearly
half of whom have had firsthand exposure to violence, suffer
from serious emotional distress, exhibiting behaviors like recur-
rent nightmares, sleeplessness, bedwetting, and aggression.

Death, disability, and psychological trauma all speak of the
insecurity resulting from violence and the threat of violence. Insecurity is one of the key factors that shapes this conflict. For Israeli Jews, the insecurity arises from a pervasive and ever-present fear of victimization. They fear being victims of a suicide
bombing, a drive-by shooting, or a sniper's attack. Many are
anxious about riding public buses, gathering in public places, or
standing at regular hitch-hiking spots.

For many Israelis, these immediate fears tap into deeper
fears about their country's viability as a nation. Despite Israel's
victory in five successive wars and its overwhelming military
might in relation to surrounding Arab nations, Israelis continue
to fear that their country could be wiped off the map. At an even
deeper level, there is also fear for Jewish survival. Having experienced centuries of anti-Judaism, massacres, and expulsions,
culminating in the *Shoah* (Holocaust), many Israeli Jews continue to experience a profound sense of vulnerability and insecurity as a result of simply being Jewish. One of the major reasons for the founding of the state of Israel was to provide a safe
place for Jewish people to live. The determination that "Never
Again!" should the horrors of the Holocaust occur leads some
Jews to emphasize the need for strength and even military
might. Other Israelis, meanwhile, point out that today Jews are
more at risk in Israel than in any other place in the world where
Jews live.[2] The Israeli sense of insecurity is profound and Israeli
longing for security is pervasive.

Palestinians also experience intense insecurity. As detailed in other chapters, thousands were made refugees in 1948, some again in 1967, and have not been able to return to their homes. Many have lived under military occupation for nearly forty years—a whole generation of Palestinians knows nothing but occupation. Many Palestinians have also experienced firsthand the killing or arrest of loved ones. They have sought shelter in their homes at night as fighter jets or helicopter gunships fired missiles overhead. They have seen their homes demolished by bulldozers before their own eyes. They have watched their children throw stones at tanks, desensitized to the danger and death that are ever-present and ever-possible. They have witnessed walls, barbed wire, and military checkpoints enclose them in ghetto-like confines. The future looks frightening and uncertain.

For Palestinians, insecurity also has to do with economics. With the loss of land and livelihood, and with life circumscribed by the occupation, many Palestinian families have found it almost impossible to make ends meet. Agriculture, the primary industry, has taken a terrible beating. Farmers have great difficulty exporting their olives, grapes, and other produce. Many cannot access their land at all. Tourism, a major source of revenue, especially for East Jerusalem and Bethlehem, has suffered greatly as ongoing violence and military closures have kept tourists away. Additionally, thousands of Palestinians from Gaza and the West Bank, who used to travel into Israel for regular jobs or casual work, are no longer able to do so. Only a fraction of Palestinians still hold the permits allowing them daily passage into Israel. Consequently, unemployment levels have soared, as have rates of poverty. Up to sixty percent of the Palestinians living in the Occupied Territories, according to the United Nations, fall below the poverty level of $2.10 dollars per day.

The construction of the separation barrier has also had a devastating economic impact on hundreds of family businesses. Locked-up shops and stores are a common sight near the barrier. Even some of the most resourceful and resilient of Palestinians have had to turn to food relief so that their children can eat. For Palestinians insecurity is not only about fear and uncertainty; it is also about poverty, deprivation, and want.

Both Israelis and Palestinians long for safety and security in the land, for freedom from want and freedom from fear. But both

Israelis and Palestinians are victims of ongoing insecurity, even as they both, to varying degrees, perpetuate it. Ironically, the pursuit of security often fuels insecurity.

RESPONDING TO INSECURITY

Israel has chosen to respond to the problem of its insecurity by building a strong military force. The support of the United States, Israel's strongest ally, is indispensable for this strategy. The U.S. provides Israel with more than $3 billion in aid annually, making it by far the largest recipient of American foreign assistance. Close to two-thirds of this $3 billion is military aid, specifically for the procurement of weapons, technology, and training. As a result Israel has achieved a level of military firepower and sophistication that is way out of proportion to its small geographic size and population. The Israeli military boasts a fleet of nearly 400 F-16 fighter jets (second in size only to the U.S.), several hundred attack helicopters, 4,000 tanks, and 11,000 other armed vehicles.[3] American military aid also provides support for Israel's own weapons industry. Today Israel is the world's tenth largest developer and exporter of arms, with some of the most sophisticated equipment in the world included among its wares.

Israeli society is highly militarized in other ways. Many Israeli political leaders, including almost all of its prime ministers, have been army officers who bring a military orientation to their understanding and practice of nation building. All young men, with limited exceptions, must perform three years of military service upon the completion of high school and must be available for reserve duty one month each year until the age of forty-five. Young women are required to serve twenty-one months. Military stories and images are a prominent part of Israeli media, culture, and education. Most Israelis grow up regarding the use of military force as a normal way of dealing with political problems.

Not surprisingly, Israel employs military means to deal with Palestinian resistance. Israeli forces regularly assassinate Palestinian militants, frequently killing or injuring unarmed civilians in the process. The Israeli military launches mortar and missile attacks on Palestinian communities believed to house militants.

Sometimes they use live ammunition against Palestinian pro-testers, sometimes against children armed only with stones. They conduct invasive night sweeps of Palestinian towns and villages, arresting scores of young men who may spend months or years in prison without charge. Due process is routinely de-nied Palestinians held in Israeli prisons, and many Palestinians face months, even years, of administrative detention without ever having charges brought against them. Israeli security strat-egy also includes heavily armed checkpoints, roadblocks, and closures, as well as the separation barrier, all of which prevent the movement of Palestinian people and goods.

Some Palestinians have also chosen violent means to re-spond to the insecurity resulting from the confiscation and occu-pation of their land. Over the years, Palestinian resistance has been primarily nonviolent—consisting of demonstrations, marches, strikes, boycotts, and other forms of non-cooperation. But a portion of the population has also taken up arms against Is-rael and against Israeli citizens. In the 1970s and 1980s, for exam-ple, the Palestine Liberation Organization endorsed armed struggle as a means of resistance, and it engaged in airplane hi-jackings and other violent activities. More recently, groups like Hamas, Islamic Jihad, and the Al-Aqsa Martyrs Brigade have waged a kind of guerrilla warfare against members of the Israeli military and civilian public alike. In the last number of years, some Palestinian militants have carried out suicide bombings targeting Israeli civilians, including children and young people. They have also increasingly launched rocket attacks from Gaza into Israel.

Both the state of Israel and certain Palestinian groups have resorted to armed force to address their respective needs for se-curity—though with levels of military capability that really can-not be compared. Ironically, the result has been not more secu-rity but more insecurity. The more firepower Israel uses and the tighter the restrictions it imposes on Palestinian communities, the more Palestinians are enraged and driven to desperate and extremist responses. Similarly, the more Palestinian militants blow up innocent Israeli civilians, the more likely Israel is to re-spond with devastating military force. The cycle of violence builds as suicide bombing leads to military assassination which leads to checkpoint attacks which leads to invasions of entire communities. Both Israelis and Palestinians long for safety and security in the land, but the very acts that are to supposed to build security only lead to more deaths and leave people on both sides more fearful and more vulnerable. Security seems ever more elusive.

NORTH AMERICAN CONNECTIONS

The Israeli-Palestinian conflict is complex and at times seems intractable. Yet North American Christians should not be quick to pass judgment on either side, for in many ways we have been part of the problem rather than the solution. First of all, many North American Christians have failed to recognize and take responsibility for the ongoing insecurity that Jews around the world experience. We have not adequately sought to understand and to resist the scourge of anti-Judaism that is still a reality in many communities.

Second, American military aid and political support is a major factor perpetuating the conflict. Without U.S. backing, Israel's confiscation of Palestinian land and the military repression of Palestinian opposition would not have reached the current crisis level. Some Christians have challenged U.S. policy, but many more support it unquestioningly. Many North American evangelicals have been among the strongest supporters of Israel's push to gain all the land of historic Palestine, viewing this as part of God's unfolding plan. These evangelicals have failed to heed the cries of Palestinians for justice and have closed their ears to the voices of Palestinian Christians who, while a distinct minority, play a vital role within Palestinian society.

Yet another way in which North American Christians are an obstacle to peace and security for Israelis and Palestinians involves our own understanding of security. Especially since September 11, 2001, many North American Christians have accepted exclusive and militaristic notions of security. We accept the notion that equates one superpower's security with global security and that what is good for the U.S. is good for all people. We regard "our way of life"—that is, our disproportionate use of the world's resources—as something that needs to be protected and preserved, even if this means that others live without the basic necessities of life. We support massive increases in military spending and a costly and deadly "war on terror" in Afghanistan and Iraq as the necessary means to ensure our safety.

While such a strategy may bring some temporary measure of physical safety for ourselves, it sets us on a dangerous trajectory. Not only does it result in death, destruction, and deprivation for others, but it also breeds alienation and anger. We are trying to ensure our own security at the expense of others, and we are doomed to fail. If Israelis and Palestinians need a different security strategy, so do we.

IMAGINING ALTERNATIVES

The Bible can be a resource for Christians seeking more redemptive and life-giving visions of security. One such vision is found in a story in 2 Kings 6. The setting is another episode in a drawn-out conflict between Israel and Aram (the Hebrew term for Syria). For a long time the Arameans have conducted murderous raids on Israel's towns and villages, and for a long time Israel has responded with violent attacks. Through the prophet Elisha's miraculous actions, the Aramean army finds itself standing, helpless and bewildered, before King Jehoram of Israel.

This is the moment when Israel could finally take revenge and put an end to the murderous Arameans. Jehoram only has to give the word and his men will slay the Aramean army. He longs to kill them—this is, after all, what nations do to their enemies. But he pauses for a moment and asks Elisha's permission, "Father, shall I kill them? Shall I kill them?" (v. 21).

Elisha responds with a most surprising command: He orders Jehoram to bring food and drink to the detained Arameans. Jehoram obeys and prepares a great feast. After the enemy soldiers have eaten, Jehoram sends them on their way. The story concludes with the words, "And the Arameans no longer came raiding into the land of Israel" (v. 22).

The text gives very little additional detail. We do not know why Elisha gives his surprising command. Perhaps he recognizes that Israel's old accepted way of dealing with the enemy is futile and doomed to failure. Perhaps he recognizes that the Arameans are humans too and thus deserve some compassion.

Perhaps he dares to believe that peace and security for Israel can be better achieved through an act of kindness and the meeting of a basic human need like hunger than through more death and destruction. We don't know Elisha's or Jehoram's thinking. We do know that both men act creatively and courageously and counter to common practice.

If we read further in 2 Kings, we learn that the Israel-Aram conflict is not completely over. Nevertheless, the simple act of feeding and giving drink to the enemy is a step toward peace and security. For a time, at least, the incursions stop. Perhaps if King Jehoram had followed up his feast with other conciliatory initiatives, a more lasting peace would have ensued. The important thing about the story is that it suggests an alternative to the accepted security strategy of retaliatory violence. It does not offer a full-blown peacebuilding strategy, but it imagines a first step out of the endless cycle of violence in which Israel and Aram are locked.[4] Interestingly, the book of Proverbs claims that wisdom is found in feeding and giving drink to enemies (25:21-22), an assertion supported by Paul in his letter to the Romans (12:14-21).

Additional alternative visions of security are found in Scripture. A familiar one, discussed briefly in chapter 7, is found in Micah 4, which dreams that

> they shall beat their swords into plowshares,
> and their spears into pruning hooks;
> nation shall not lift up sword against nation,
> neither shall they learn war any more;
> but they shall all sit under their own vines and under
>   their own fig trees,
> and no one shall make them afraid;
> for the mouth of the Lord of hosts has spoken.
> —Micah 4:3b-4

In this comforting image, the nations have ceased to wage war against one another and have turned their weapons into farm tools. Farmers live on their own land, caring for their own vines and fig trees. The land presumably provides food and income for them. No one threatens another with dispossession, displacement, or violence. The nations live without want and without fear.

The vision presented in this text is striking in a number of ways. First, the security it portrays is inclusive—it embraces "the nations." Security is not just for Israel; it is for all peoples. Security for one is linked to security for all. Second, the text recognizes that security blossoms when weapons are converted into life-giving tools, and even the "learning" of war is abandoned. The nations not only stop their warring, but they also undergo a process of disarmament and demilitarization, so that they no longer possess the war-making arsenal or know-how. In this way they can no longer threaten one another. Finally, the vision includes the economic security that results when people have unthreatened access to land and a source of livelihood. Peace without the means to put food on the table is a shallow peace.

Certain texts from the book of Isaiah also address the theme of security, with a particular focus on justice. Chapter 32, for instance, imagines kings and princes who will rule with justice and righteousness and who will thereby provide safety and security for their people (32:2). On the day when God's spirit is poured out, (32:15-16), justice and righteousness will live in the land, making the wilderness a fruitful field and the fruitful field a forest. The result of justice and righteousness will be peace and security for all.

> The effect of righteousness will be peace,
> and the result of righteousness, quietness
>   and trust forever.
> My people will abide in a peaceful habitation,
> in secure dwellings, and in quiet resting places.
> —Isaiah 32:17-18

These brief Scripture texts from 2 Kings, Micah, and Isaiah imagine security in ways that provide alternatives to the logic of violence so pervasive in our twenty-first century world. They envision a different kind of strategy—a strategy that involves addressing the needs and concerns of enemies, pursuing justice and right relations, rejecting weapons and warfare, and living in peaceful coexistence.

The Bible therefore can help us discern an alternative security strategy to the logic of violence. At the same time, it is important to acknowledge that some biblical passages pertaining to security are very troublesome. As we have seen, some Scripture texts suggest that Israel's security in biblical times was to be found in slaughtering its enemies. Some texts in fact claim that God would be the divine warrior who would take care of the grisly job on Israel's behalf (see Exod. 15). Others simply portray a narrow concept of security—one that assumed that Israel's security could be obtained at the expense of others' security. It is important for us to recognize that the Scriptures do not speak with one voice on this topic, and it is necessary for faithful Christians to discern which passages more faithfully reflect the God whose love, justice, and salvation extends to all people.

ISRAELIS AND PALESTINIANS BUILDING PEACE

Many Israelis and Palestinians recognize that current security strategies have proven disastrous. They are calling for a change of course. They realize that injustice breeds anger and rage and that desperate acts and violence beget more violence. They insist that security must be built step by step, as ongoing injustices experienced by Palestinians are addressed, and as violence and armed force on the part of both Israelis and Palestinians are rejected. Although many of these peacemakers do not claim the Judeo-Christian tradition and therefore do not turn to the Bible for guidance on matters of security, they are nevertheless helping to imagine and to implement the kind of alternative vision described in the Scripture texts identified above.

Among these peacebuilders are Robi Damelin and Elham Elshoabe, mentioned at the beginning of this chapter. Due to having lost sons to the conflict, Robi and Elham have joined an organization called the Families Forum. Families Forum brings together people, both Israeli and Palestinian, who have lost loved ones and seeks to build understanding through dialogue and the sharing of stories. Members of the group visit schools and community groups to try to break down the fears and the stereotypes people may have about one another. They insist that this kind of human interaction and relationship-building, rather than military offensives, will enhance security for Israelis and Palestinians. They also advocate for an end to the occupation and for addressing the grievances of Palestinians.

Dorothy Naor is part of an Israeli group called New Profile which also seeks to build security through peaceful means.

Dorothy was a longtime supporter of Israeli government policies until autumn 2000, when Israeli soldiers shot and killed thirteen Palestinian citizens of Israel who were participating in nonviolent demonstrations. She began to question the pervasive militarization of Israeli life and the notion that war and military repression are inevitable and acceptable ways of solving problems. Today Dorothy and her colleagues at New Profile promote nonviolent conflict resolution, the right to conscientious objection, and the demilitarization of education and culture. With respect to Palestine, New Profile says that Israel must cease being an occupying nation and must become a respectful neighbor. According to Dorothy, "Israelis will have no security until Palestinians have it too."[5]

Mitri Raheb also understands that security is rooted in justice and right relations between Israelis and Palestinians. Mitri is pastor of the Christmas Lutheran Church in Bethlehem. He is a Palestinian who is outspoken in denouncing Israeli oppression but committed to the way of nonviolent resistance. He and others from his community have sought to strengthen Palestinian culture and identity through initiatives for children, youth, and adults. In 2002 Israeli soldiers, with tanks and helicopter gunships, invaded the town of Bethlehem and placed it under siege for many weeks. Mitri's home and church as well as neighboring buildings were damaged by tanks and mortar shells. At one point Mitri ventured from his home into the courtyard of the church to see the extent of the damage. Soldiers surrounded him and pointed a gun to his head. When one of them taunted him by calling him a wise guy, he responded, "The real wise person is he who can transform his enemy into a neighbor, and not his neighbor into an enemy."[6]

A WAY FORWARD

Are there ways North American Christians can support more life-giving strategies so Israelis and Palestinians can experience genuine security and become neighbors? Is it possible for us to participate in efforts that stop the cycle of violence and nurture initiatives that build true security for both peoples?

A starting point is confession. As already indicated, North American Christians are in many ways part of the problem that perpetuates insecurity for Israelis and Palestinians and other members of the human family. It is wrong for us to call Palestinians and Israelis to lay down their weapons and practice justice unless we are prepared to do the same. Before we do anything else, we must examine our understandings and expectations with respect to security and confess ways they have contributed to violence and suffering for others.

Second, North American Christians can learn about and support those groups of Israelis and Palestinians, mentioned above, who are already working to build security in the land through justice, right relations, and nonviolent peacebuilding. Mainstream Western media are predisposed to report on those Palestinians who commit suicide bombings and Israelis who retaliate with military might. This is an incomplete picture. It is important for North Americans to support and share the stories of those groups of committed people, on both sides of the conflict, who are building security by reaching out to the other side.

Third, North American Christians can help to imagine creative alternatives for building security that are grounded in the ways of peace, justice, and inclusion. We do not have all the answers and we must always speak with humility. But we can articulate the kind of vision of security exemplified in the biblical texts noted above. We can advocate for security policies that address longstanding injustices, build economic well-being, limit the resort to violent force, and encourage creative conflict resolution. We can promote the idea that security in the land of Palestine-Israel can only be gained through addressing the security needs of both peoples. We can resist the commonly accepted wisdom and practice that security can be built through weapons and walls and systems of oppression. We can dare to dream that a way to security is through laying down weapons and feeding the enemy.

The massive separation wall that encircles Bethlehem has been decorated with much graffiti. One piece of advice scrawled on the wall and directed to Israel's government says, "Give them justice, and they will reward you with peace." It is not unlike Elijah's command to King Jehoram to feed the Aramean army. In the context of security strategies that compound insecurity, this simple advice points a hopeful and life-giving way toward security that ensures freedom from fear and freedom from want.

QUESTIONS FOR DISCUSSION

1. How would you identify the physical, psychological, and economic aspects of security, both personal and collective? What other factors contribute to security and insecurity?

2. What are some additional biblical resources, besides the texts from 2 Kings, Micah, and Isaiah, that can help Christians in seeking security?

3. In Romans 12, Paul urges the Christians in Rome to respond to evil with good and to give food and drink to enemies. His counsel is similar to Jesus' command to his followers to love their enemies and do good to those who hate them. Is this an ethic for Christians only? Is it an ethic that Christians can ask of their state or society?

SUGGESTION FOR ACTION

This chapter identified three different ways that North American Christians can promote security for Israelis and Palestinians. How do you respond to these suggestions? What are some specific policies that Canadians and Americans might advocate with their governments? What additional ways can North American Christians be part of the solution rather than part of the problem? Contact the MCC offices in Ottawa or Washington, D.C. for more ideas about how to advocate for just peace in Palestine-Israel.

NOTES

1. Statistics from B'Tselem: The Israeli Information Centre for Human Rights in the Occupied Territories, www.btselem.org/english/statistics/Casualties.asp. Accessed on December 14, 2005.

2. This comment was made by Dorothy Naor of New Profile, an Israeli organization promoting the demilitarization of Israeli society, at the Intercultural Conference on Land, Peoples and Identities, Bethlehem, November 6-12, 2005.

3. Statistics are from Jewish Institute for National Security Affairswww.jinsa.org/articles/articles.html/function/view/categoryid/154/documentid/2291/history/3,2360,654,154,2291, and Sharon Komash, "Israel's Military Industrial Complex," at www.monitor.upeace.org/pdf/israel.pdf. Accessed December 15, 2005.

4. Titus Peachey, "The First Step Toward Peace: A Reflection on 2 Kings 6," *Pathway A, Second Mile: A Peace Journey for Congregations* (Scottdale, Pa.: Mennonite Publishing House, 2002).

5. This comment was made at the Intercultural Conference on Land, Peoples and Identities, Bethlehem, November 6-12, 2005. New Profile's website is newprofile.org.

6. Mitri Raheb, *Bethlehem Besieged* (Maryknoll, N.Y.: Orbis Books, 2004), 22.

Chapter 9

The Land in
the End Times: Part I

Dan Epp-Tiessen

*I*n November 2005, American pastor and televangelist John Hagee made another of his frequent trips to Israel. Hagee makes a point of meeting every new Israeli prime minister, and his congregation actively supports the state of Israel.[1] Again on this trip Hagee met with leading Israeli politicians and delivered a speech at the Knesset, the Israeli parliament. The printed version of the speech released to the media states, "We believe God owns the land and has deeded it to the Jewish people—a deed that cannot be canceled or amended—not by the road map to peace, not by the EU [European Union], not even by the president of the United States." "I do not consider it an accident that the very same week Jews were driven out of Gaza and placed in tent cities in Israel, the hand of God, through Hurricane Katrina, drove Americans out of their homes to live in tent cities in America."[2]

Gaza is a thin strip of land along the Mediterranean Sea where 1.5 million Palestinians are crammed into 140 square miles (ca. 363 square km). Yet 5,000 Jewish settlers had taken over 30 percent of the best farmland and beachfront real estate in Gaza. Dismantling the Jewish settlements was a small act of justice correcting an earlier injustice. Hagee may be somewhat extreme in his views, but a host of evangelical publications and

websites proclaim that Israel has a divine mandate to occupy all
of Palestine and must relinquish no part of it.

One reason so many Christians enthusiastically support Israel is that they see the creation of the state of Israel as a key step
in God's roadmap for the last days. According to the popular
end-times scenario, the restoration of Israel is the most important biblical sign that must fall into place before the faithful are
raptured, Jesus returns in triumph, and God's kingdom conquers all evil. Without the state of Israel, none of God's end-time
events are possible. With the creation of the state of Israel, these
events will assuredly unfold in the near future. Therefore, to
challenge Israel's methods of acquiring and holding the land is
to oppose the plans of God.

Alex Awad is an unabashed evangelical Palestinian Christian who pastors the East Jerusalem Baptist church and teaches
at Bethlehem Bible College. He believes that many Christian
end-times scenarios are dangerous. He cites his own spiritual
pilgrimage to illustrate. There was a time when he believed the
typical scenarios, and so he rejoiced when he saw media reports
of wars, earthquakes, famines, and other catastrophes. Had not
Jesus proclaimed that such disasters were harbingers of the end
(Luke 21:9-11)? Therefore, the more disasters and human suffering, the closer we supposedly were to the rapture and the coming of God's kingdom. Now Awad sees things very differently.
All Christian beliefs about the end of the world must pass
through the cross of Christ, he asserts. Any Christian teaching
about the end must be consistent with the overall life, ministry,
death, and resurrection of Christ—all of which demonstrate
God's desire for the wellbeing of human beings and not their destruction.

Awad observes that it easy to spell out end-times scenarios
in books and movies, but in real life these scenarios are sometimes implemented in blood. Alex cites the words of Jesus, "you
will know them by their fruits" (Matt. 7:20). The fruit of many
end-times scenarios is to render invisible or inconsequential the
suffering of the Palestinian people. End-times writers claim that
the state of Israel is necessary in God's plan; therefore it deserves
our unqualified support. Israel's oppression of the Palestinians
and its acquisition of ever more Palestinian land are either overlooked or justified as necessary to fulfill God's plans.

Awad is a gentle man, so he is quick to add that most ordinary Christians who accept end-times scenarios are well-intentioned people, but they are unaware of the consequences of their beliefs and actions.

A BRIEF HISTORY OF
CHRISTIAN END-TIMES BELIEFS

The Bible, especially the New Testament, expresses lively convictions that God will bring human life and history to a meaningful end. Therefore it is not surprising that church history is populated with individuals and groups who were preoccupied with discerning the signs and times of that end. Numerous biblical interpreters have even dared to be more or less specific in their predictions regarding the time of the end. So far they and their followers have always been disappointed. Even in the modern era, Hal Lindsey writing in 1970 suggested that the end could arrive in forty years after 1948, when the state of Israel was founded.[3] His projected date of 1988 is now distant memory.

Although earlier eras such as the Protestant Reformation sometimes witnessed intense expectations that the end was near, these expectations took different forms than contemporary end-times scenarios. For example, until the nineteenth century there was no expectation that the restoration of Israel was essential for the return of Christ and the final establishment of God's kingdom. The basic outline of contemporary end-times scenarios was first worked out and popularized in the middle of the nineteenth century by an Irish evangelical pastor named John Nelson Darby. One of the new elements of end-times scenarios since Darby is the conviction that Old Testament passages foretelling the restoration of Israel must be fulfilled literally, and that a new Jewish state is a pre-condition for other end-times events. Before Darby, most Christians paid little attention to such texts. Instead they took their cues from the New Testament—which makes no mention of a restored Jewish state as part of God's plan for the future.

The credibility of the new end-times scenario received a major boost with the return of large numbers of Jews to Palestine and the eventual establishment of the state of Israel in 1948. Events seemed to be unfolding just as some biblical interpreters had predicted. As the twentieth century progressed, end-times scenarios became increasingly popular in North American evangelicalism. The movement mushroomed after the publication in 1970 of Hal Lindsey's *The Late Great Planet Earth*, which has by now sold over thirty-five million copies. This book and many others like it convince millions of readers that contemporary events are unfolding according to a script prophesied long ago in the Bible. In recent years, promoting end times scenarios has become a huge business, as evidenced by an endless stream of books, television and radio shows, movies, and web sites dedicated to the signs of the end.

THE COMMON END-TIMES SCENARIO

Although there is some variation in the scenarios, the basic end-times picture runs something like this. As the end approaches, attentive believers will witness fulfillment of signs predicted by the Bible: an upsurge of natural disasters like earthquakes, famines and epidemics, increasing immorality and ungodliness, wars and rumors of wars, persecution and martyrdom of Christians, and proclamation of the gospel to all nations.

In addition to these more general signs, specific political developments are unfolding on the world stage as prophesied long ago. Chief among these is the restoration of the state of Israel, in fulfillment of Old Testament promises that God will gather the Jews from exile. Because this is such a key event in starting the final countdown to the end, many evangelicals are not content to be mere observers of the unfolding end-times script. They offer financial assistance and unqualified support to the state of Israel as a way to participate in the fulfillment of God's plans.

Other specific developments in the end-times countdown include the formation of the European Union, which ensures that there is a revived Roman Empire of ten nations as supposedly spelled out in Daniel 7:24 and Revelation 13:1. China's rise to power means that it will provide the great army of 200 million cavalry from the east that will march on the Holy Land (Rev. 9:13-19; 16:12). Despite the breakup of the Soviet Union, Russia is still large and powerful enough to fill the role of Gog and Magog, the mighty enemy from the north that will attack Israel (Ezek. 38-39). The end-times literature asserts that since the key signs are now in place, the final countdown has begun and the world is rapidly moving towards its end.

End-times interpreters assure Christians that there is no need to be anxious about the momentous events and catastrophes soon to unfold, because Christians will only be around long enough to observe the stage being set and the actors taking their places. Before the world sinks into utter chaos, the rapture will occur—God's trumpet will sound, Jesus will return, and true Christians will meet him in the air, then be whisked off to heaven (1 Thess. 4:16-17).

Shortly after the rapture, a great world leader will arise. For three-and-a-half years he will bring peace, order, and prosperity to the world, and he will make a special covenant with Israel to protect her from all foes. After this initial honeymoon period, the world leader will reveal his true colors and prove to be the great antichrist. He will break his covenant with Israel, demand to be worshiped, and for the next three-and-a-half years carry on a reign of terror against all who refuse to accept his pretensions— especially Jews, other minorities, and any persons who have turned to Christ after the rapture. Some writers assert that during this period the Jews will turn to Christ (cf. Rom. 11:25-32) and will face persecution even worse than under Hitler.

The last half of the world dictator's rule will see God unleash the terrible judgments vividly described in Revelation 6-18. Epidemics, earthquakes, war, and cosmic upheaval will devastate the world during this period called the Great Tribulation. Human-made and natural disasters will combine to create unimaginable suffering and reduce the world's population to a fraction of what it is now. Sometime during the antichrist's reign, Russia (Gog of Ezek. 38-39) will make one last attempt to attack Israel and gain power over the Middle East. God will intervene to defend Israel and wipe out the Russian armies.

The time of tribulation and chaos will climax in the great battle of Armageddon (Rev. 16:16).[4] Hundreds of millions of troops from European nations in the north, African nations in the south, and China in the east, will converge on Israel to participate in the world's biggest battle ever. Some will fight for and some against the antichrist. Before the outcome of the battle is determined, Jesus will return with his angels and saints to utterly annihilate all these armies in the climactic battle of Armageddon.

The antichrist and his followers will be thrown into a lake of fire. Satan will be bound and cast into a bottomless pit. With the evil powers out of the way, Christ will initiate the millennium, a thousand year reign of peace and well-being (Rev. 20:4-15). The good times will end when Satan is released for a short period, allowing him to lead one last rebellion against God. But God will quickly defeat Satan, this time once and for all.

Then God will resurrect all the dead and convene the last judgment to decide the eternal destiny of every human being. After everyone has been assigned to their proper place in heaven or hell, God will create a new heaven and a new earth as an eternal home for the faithful.

QUESTIONS ABOUT THE SCENARIO

Which biblical book actually spells out this rather complex series of events leading up to the end? Actually, none does. End-times interpreters range widely across the Bible, especially the books of Ezekiel, Daniel, and Revelation, gathering texts and images relating to the restoration of Israel, the coming of God's kingdom, and the end of the world. The collected pieces of information are then combined into one grand scheme and the various events placed into a supposed chronological order.

This is what we might call "cut-and-paste interpretation" of the Bible. Many computer users find the cut-and-paste command to be one of the computer's most useful features. One can begin with many different documents, cut numerous snippets of text from each, and paste them into an entirely new document, creating a scrapbook of materials copied from elsewhere. The new document might be interesting and even edifying, but we would not claim that such a composite work reflects the mind of each of the original documents. Most end-times specialists function as cut-and-paste interpreters. They work with biblical materials, but their scenarios are human creations that do not reflect the vision of any one biblical book or author.

An apparent strength of end-times interpreters is their extensive use of the Bible, giving the impression that their work has a solid biblical foundation. However, we would not say that the person who created the cut-and-paste document is offering a thorough and careful interpretation of the texts from which he or she has extracted material. A fundamental principle of faithful biblical interpretation (and interpretation of any other texts as well) is that individual passages should first of all be interpreted in light of their own context. With respect to what the Bible says about the future, it is important to study each passage and biblical book carefully and discern what message or vision each writer sought to communicate about the future. Then it is appropriate and helpful to compare the vision of individual books with other biblical perspectives. To compile a composite scenario created out of hundreds of texts gleaned from all over the Bible, then proclaim it as the biblical roadmap to the end, is to create a human edifice and impose it on the individual biblical texts.

End-times scenarios place considerable emphasis on the supposedly increasing chaos and degeneration afflicting the natural and human world. We are supposed to interpret such afflictions as signs that the end is nigh. Alex Awad points out that such interpretations can be dangerous, because they encourage us to welcome disaster and to be passive in the face of evil and suffering. If God's plan is for the world to sink into ever greater chaos, then promoting peace and justice and caring for the environment place us in opposition to God. End-times interpreters frequently disparage human efforts to work for reconciliation and healing in the Middle East as a waste of time and energy. Such thinking flies directly in the face of the Bible's consistent call for God's people to resist all forms of sin, evil, and injustice. Awad's caution is worth remembering, since "by their fruits you shall know them."

A central feature of end-times speculation is the assertion that the end is just around the corner, and that therefore Christians ought to be attentive to the signs of the times. The prevalence of end-times books, movies, and web-sites may create an environment in which preoccupation with the end is out of proportion to what is healthy for a well-rounded Christian life.

In Jesus' time it was not unusual to be preoccupied with looking for signs of the arrival of God's kingdom, as is evident from the amount of end-times literature that emerged from his era. Jesus was familiar with such expectations and also described for his followers some of the signs of the end (Mark 13 and the parallel passages in Matt. 24 and Luke 21). But at the conclusion of his instructions he was careful to add a caution, stressing that no one knows the exact time, not the angels, not even he himself, but only God (Mark 13:32; Matt. 24:36). Jesus cautioned that since we can never know the exact time of the end, there is not much to be gained by speculating. We do much better to devote our energies to watchful and faithful living, working on behalf of the kingdom, so that it does not matter if we are surprised by his return (Mark 13:33-37; Matt. 24:45-51; 25:1-30).

HOW TO INTERPRET END-TIMES PASSAGES

A key issue in the end-times discussion is how we read and interpret biblical texts about the future. As a way of exploring this question, I want to reflect on the Bible's teaching about another kind of end—namely, the end of our human lives. The end of our individual lives is not unrelated to the end of the world, in that both relate to God's ultimate plans for human existence. The word *end* has a double meaning here—end as in the chronological end of our earthly lives, and end as in the ultimate purpose and outcome of our lives.

The New Testament uses a variety of images to speak about the "end" of our lives. One central image is resurrection of the body. Originally, ancient Israelites had no belief in a meaningful life after death, but late in the Old Testament period Jews came to believe that God would never abandon the faithful, not even in death. In Israelite thought a human being was one indivisible entity, so Jews envisioned the new life God would grant after death as a resurrection of the body. This image stands in contrast to the ancient Greek understanding of a human being as consisting of body and spirit. At death the two parted company and the body decayed while the immortal spirit continued to live on in the life hereafter.

Resurrection of the body is a central image in the New Testament. God raised Jesus from the dead. This is not just a spiritual resurrection. The New Testament stresses that the tomb is empty and that the resurrected Jesus has a body that eats (Luke 24:41-43) and can be touched (Luke 24:39; John 20:27). Paul interprets the resurrection of Jesus as God's promise that someday the followers of Jesus will experience a similar resurrection of their bodies (1 Cor. 15:12-23).

How literally should we interpret resurrection? The human body consists of somewhere around sixty percent water. When I die and am buried, the millions of water molecules in my body will be released into the underground water table. Some will flow into rivers and lakes, become drinking water for someone else, and as a result become part of another person's body. In the day of resurrection, from where will God retrieve the molecules to resurrect my body?

This question illustrates how literal interpretations can become ridiculous when pushed too far. One time the Sadducees attempted to discredit Jesus' convictions about resurrection with just such a literal interpretation. They told a story of a woman who had a series of seven husbands during her life, and then asked Jesus which of the seven would be her husband in the resurrection. Jesus chided the Sadducees for their literalism, stating "For when they rise from the dead, they neither marry nor are given in marriage. . ." (Mark 12:25). Jesus' response indicates that resurrection of the dead is an image of the new life God will grant us after death, and that we should avoid literal interpretations which assume that our bodily life in the next world will be just like our bodily life in the present. Paul makes the same point in 1 Corinthians 15:35-49, stressing that life in our resurrected body will be qualitatively different than life in our current body.

The image of resurrection has become extremely meaningful to me after the death of our eight-year-old son Tim some years ago. From birth on Tim struggled with a variety of health problems and disabilities. At age three he required surgery, chemotherapy, and radiation to treat a large brain tumor. The treatments and their side effects left him quite limited physically and mentally and robbed him of his vision. Five years later the cancer recurred and claimed Tim's body.

Tim has now experienced resurrection. He enjoys a new body. He can run and jump and play with other children like he never could before. Tim can see again and is delighting in the flowers and picture books in heaven. Is all this literally true? Does Tim still have the body of a child? Or are these comments about Tim's resurrection images of the healing and new life God will some day grant us?

Alongside the older belief in the resurrection of the body, the New Testament also reflects ideas borrowed from Greek thought about humans having an immortal soul that lives on after the body dies and decays. Jesus says to the thief on the cross, "Truly I tell you, today you will be with me in Paradise" (Luke 23:43). Throughout most of church history, the Greek view of the immortal soul has informed Christian belief more so than the image of resurrection. I have generally been more attracted to the Jewish image of the resurrection of the body, partly because I appreciate how this image affirms the importance of our bodies and earthly life. But when Tim died, the image of an immortal soul acquired new power for me. Holding Tim's lifeless body, it was evident that the body was there, but the "real" Tim was elsewhere. His soul is now in the loving presence of God. This too is a powerful image of the new life God has in store for us.

We should not be surprised that the New Testament uses a variety of images as it seeks to portray what life after death will be like. None of us has yet experienced this life. How else can we portray it except by using images that provide but partial glimpses of what life will be like in God's glorious presence? Both Jesus and Paul caution us that to interpret these images literally is to misunderstand and distort the reality to which they point.

Perhaps biblical language about the end of the world (*end* again with the double meaning of both chronological end and end as purpose or outcome) is best understood as functioning like the New Testament language about life after death. The Bible uses a multitude of images to assert that history is ultimately in God's hands, that some day the kingdom Jesus inaugurated at his first coming will be brought to completion at his second coming, and that some day God will deal in a final and appropriate way with evil. To expect literal fulfillment of all biblical texts that speak about the end of the world is like interpreting passages about life after death in a strictly literal way.

Literal language is simply not rich or varied enough to adequately grasp such important realities and to speak of things which we humans can but see in a mirror dimly (1 Cor. 13:12). That is why so many of the biblical texts about God's future draw from a large pool of figurative language and symbols that were familiar during biblical times. Some of this symbolic language now strikes us as strange and perhaps even bizarre, because it is no longer part of our common stock of language and images. Recognizing how the Bible often uses figurative language should caution us against strictly literal interpretations of end-times passages that were never intended to be understood literally.

The classic rapture text, for example, is 1 Thessalonians 4:16-17. Is the main point of the text that God has a trumpet in heaven that will sound forth across the universe, that Jesus will physically descend from heaven which is located above us, that believers both living and dead will physically rise to meet Christ in the clouds above the earth? Or is the main goal of the passage to assure Christians that even believers who have already died will receive the reward of resurrection (4:13) and to encourage believers facing persecution (3:1-5; 4:18) by assuring them that some day their suffering will end, Jesus will return, God's reign will come, and God will reward the faithful with resurrection?

CENTRAL THEMES OF
BIBLICAL END-TIME PASSAGES

The Bible contains a wealth of passages which speak about God's final plans for the world. Space permits only a brief summary of some of the major themes emerging from these texts that can guide our thinking about the end. The basic conviction underlying all biblical visions of the future is that in the end God's forces of good will triumph. Despite all human, natural, and supernatural forces in this world that create enormous devastation and human suffering, in the end God's reign will be fully established; there will be no more evil and suffering.

The end-times will witness the return of Christ to complete the work he initiated during his first coming. During his earthly life Jesus inaugurated the kingdom of God through his ministry of healing, casting out demons, and proclaiming the good news of God's love, grace, and peace. These signs of the kingdom are a foretaste of what Jesus will accomplish when he returns in glory to complete the work begun during his first coming.

The power of the anti-godly forces described in Revelation, Daniel, and elsewhere testifies to the tenacity and depth of evil in this world. Evil is not to be taken lightly or underestimated. But the promise of resurrection and the promise that God's kingdom will triumph function as powerful encouragement to persist in faithfulness in the midst of hardship, discouragement, and persecution, even during times when evil seems to gain the upper hand.

Underlying many passages is the conviction that our human actions are ultimately significant. God will convene a last judgment when each of us will be called to give account for our lives. Faithfulness in things big and small matters and will be rewarded with resurrection and new life. Wickedness and rebellion against God will be punished and no longer tolerated. Exactly how God will deal with evil and evildoers is not ours to determine, but we can be assured that God will do so appropriately.

Because we do not know the day or the hour, we need not be overly preoccupied with speculating about the signs and times of the end. Our calling is to immerse ourselves in the work of the kingdom so that at any moment we are prepared to meet our Lord and Maker.

Last year in the preaching course I teach, a student chose as the text for his practice sermon Revelation 21:1-4, a wonderful passage describing God's new heaven and new earth. Instead of seeking to discern at what point in the end-times calendar the heavenly Jerusalem will descend (21:2) or how God will make the hostile sea disappear (21:1), Dale described how as a young child he watched his mother rock in her chair, open Bible in her lap, tears in her eyes, reading these verses. Dale had an older brother with severe disabilities, and sometimes life became overwhelming for his mother.

Dale's mother did not look to this text to find a roadmap for her future or the future of the world. She looked to this text for assurance that the future was ultimately in God's hands, that God was with her, and that she was part of God's precious people (21:3), that some day God would wipe every tear from her eyes, and bring an end to all crying and pain, and even death would be no more (21:4). Perhaps Dale and his mother understand something of how the biblical writers intended their words about the future to be heard and appropriated.

QUESTIONS FOR DISCUSSION

1. How much attention should Christians devote to end-times issues (keeping in mind the double meaning of end as

chronological end and goal or purpose)? Does your congregation devote too little or too much attention to God's future?

2. Of the biblical texts referred to in this chapter or others not mentioned, which should play key roles in Christian thinking about the future? How do you and your church community interpret these passages?

3. How do you respond to Alex Awad's comments regarding Christian beliefs about the end-times? Do you see any dangers in popular Christian end-times thinking?

4. Are biblical texts about God's future intended to make us passive and look for God to control the course of events? Or are such passages a call to live now already in light of the future promised by God? What impact should our beliefs about the end have on how we live in the present?

SUGGESTIONS FOR ACTION

1. Encourage thoughtful reflection in your congregation about God's future and how that future ought to shape how we live in the present.

2. Pray that the Palestinian people will not be overlooked or victimized as a result of Christian end-times thinking.

NOTES

1. See the John Hagee Ministries website at www.jhm.org.

2. Cited by Lily Galili, "Rapture—or Raptor?" *Haaretz* (Nov. 11, 2005), B3.

3. *The Late Great Planet Earth* (Grand Rapids: Zondervan, 1970), 54.

4. Armageddon, meaning mountain of Megiddo, is a rather unpretentious hill in northern Israel that saw numerous battles in ancient times because it was the site of Megiddo, a town guarding the main trading route where it passed through a range of hills.

Chapter 10

The Land in the End Times: Part II

Dan Epp-Tiessen

One of the core objectives of the International Christian Embassy in Jerusalem is "to be part of God's great purposes in bringing the Jews back to Israel. 'See, I will beckon to the Gentiles, I will lift up my banner to the peoples; they will bring your sons in their arms and carry your daughters on their shoulders' (Isa. 49:22)."[1]

John Hagee Ministries declares that "As Christians, we must recognize the critical importance of the Jewish people in God's plan for us all. We must, in direct fulfillment of Jeremiah's prophecy, help bring God's people home to Israel."[2]

Both the websites quoted above encourage Christians to actively participate in what they perceive as God's fulfillment of prophecy. The second specifically invites participation in its "Exodus II" campaign, an effort to raise funds in support of Jews relocating to Israel. By making a financial contribution readers can actually "be a part of the fulfillment of prophecy."

Jean Zaru, a Palestinian Christian from Ramallah, speaks with deep pain in her voice about Christian Zionism. Inspired by her Christian faith, Zaru has for decades engaged in nonviolent resistance to the Israeli occupation of the West Bank. Evangelical Christians from North America have accused her of standing in the way of God's purposes, because she resists Israel's efforts to take over the whole land of Palestine. Zaru tells stories of Christians coming to Palestine and telling Palestinians that they should sell their land to the Jews and leave, because God's plan is to give the entire land to the Jewish people.

CHANGING CHRISTIAN VIEWS

As indicated in the prior chapter, many Christians support the state of Israel as a way to prepare the world for the end times. Some Christian groups, like the International Christian Embassy in Jerusalem, operate with end-times agenda in the background but focus their publicity on participation in the fulfillment of biblical prophecies about the return of the Jewish people from exile.

Virtually all Christians living before the middle of the nineteenth century would have regarded Christian support for a Jewish state to be both odd and unbiblical. After all, the New Testament makes no explicit reference to the restoration of a Jewish state as being part of God's plans for the future. Old Testament prophecies regarding the restoration of Israel were generally spiritualized and applied to the life of the church. The church believed that in Old Testament times God worked with the people of Israel and granted them the promises of salvation, but under the new covenant initiated by Jesus, God's salvation was offered to all humanity and was no longer linked to one people or one land. The church was the "new Israel," and biblical promises related to Israel now applied to the church.

The increasing popularity of end-times scenarios over the 150 years has led to a major shift in thinking within the evangelical wing of the church. Many evangelicals now believe that prophecies regarding the restoration of Israel should not be applied to the church. Rather, they argue that these prophecies remained unfulfilled for centuries, but now God is fulfilling them through the creation of the state of Israel.

This fulfillment is of enormous significance, because without the state of Israel, Jesus cannot return and God's kingdom remains but a far-off dream. Given these conclusions, the next step is to assert that we Christians ought to do more than passively watch prophecy unfold before our eyes; we should actively engage in ensuring its fulfillment, be it assisting with the immigration of Jews to the land of Israel or lobbying the U.S. government not to pressure Israel into making any territorial compromises.

OLD TESTAMENT PROMISES OF RESTORATION

God's promise to restore the Jewish people after destruction and exile is one of the most frequent promises found in the Old Testament regarding the future of God's people. Such promises appear in many prophetic books (Isa. 11:11-16; 35:8-10; 43:1-7; Jer. 23:3-8; 29:10-14; 30:10-22; 31:1-17; Ezek. 28:25-26; 34:11-31; chs. 36, 37, 40-48; Hos. 1:10-11; 11:10-11; Amos 9:11-15; Zech. 1:14-17; 8:1-8, 10:8-12). Most of these promises were given shortly before the destruction of the nation in 586 BCE, or shortly after this catastrophe when Jews were in Babylonian exile. The prophets who delivered these promises were speaking to a specific group of people amid a historical and spiritual crisis. This crisis threatened their faith to its core, and the prophecies of restoration must be understood in this context.

At the center of Israelite faith was the conviction that the Israelites were God's chosen people who enjoyed divine blessing, favor, and protection like no other nation. There were a few prophets around uttering threatening words about God's overwhelming judgment as punishment for Israel's unfaithfulness to God and its oppression of the poor and needy, but these prophets did not have much of a following.

Most of the people were not prepared for the Babylonian destruction of the nation and the spiritual crisis it precipitated. Besides experiencing military defeat, looting, incredible loss of life, and destruction of the nation's infrastructure, the Israelites lost the core elements of their faith in one fell swoop. Gone were the holy city of Jerusalem and the temple representing God's earthly dwelling place. Gone were the king appointed by God, the priesthood and sacrificial system, and the Promised Land. In addition, in the ancient world it was widely believed that the power of a nation was directly related to the power of its deity. Did not the enemy's victory demonstrate that the Babylonian God Marduk was far more powerful than Israel's God?

This background illustrates that one of the main purposes of the promises of restoration was to assure Israel that God had not abandoned her as some of the exiles believed (cf. Isa. 40:27; Ezek. 37:11). Despite the grim circumstances of the present, God's ultimate will was not the destruction but the restoration of Israel. In this regard the prophetic ministry of Ezekiel is instructive. Up until the Babylonian destruction of Jerusalem, he warned people of impending doom. Once the disaster unfolded, his calling shifted. He began to proclaim promises of restoration and renewal as a way of comforting and reassuring the devastated exiles, so that they would not lose hope and give up the faith.

Another important effect of the promises of restoration was to convince the people that they were indeed in exile. Exile involves physical dislocation and also a psychological choice. My father's family fled the Soviet Union shortly after the Communist revolution. My father was dislocated, but he never experienced himself as being in exile, because he had no desire to return to the Soviet Union and live under Stalin's tyranny. The prophetic promise of restoration served to remind the exiles that they were in fact in exile. They were not where they finally belonged, because God had plans for them back in the Promised Land. Thus they should be prepared to return when the time was ripe.

How important this was is illustrated by the fact that when the Babylonian empire was defeated and the Jews permitted to return, a large number chose to remain in Babylon and enjoy the comforts of their new home rather than endure the risks and rigors of return to the land of Israel. When delivering their promises of restoration, the prophets had no intention of predicting events some 2,500 years in the future. They were responding to a physical and spiritual crisis in their own time.

Typical end-times scenarios claim that God's promises of Israel's restoration refer to what will happen in the end times. By insisting on a supposedly literal fulfillment of biblical texts, such interpreters seem to "out-Bible" other interpreters who opt for a different approach. However, the literalists overlook a key feature of the Old Testament promises. While these passages look forward to a time of deliverance for God's people, they do not link this time with the end of the world, the end of human history, the rapture, or Armageddon. The point of these passages is that God will restore Israel to the land so that she can live peacefully, joyfully, and faithfully within the bounds of human history. End-times interpreters do these texts an injustice by reading features into them which are not there.

Moreover, if we read these texts carefully, we observe that they include many details which indicate that the modern state of Israel is not a literal fulfillment of these passages. Isaiah 11:16 and 35:8 both speak of the exiles returning via a special highway; Jeremiah 23:3-8 and Ezekiel 37:24-25 envision a Davidic king ruling over the restored nation; Jeremiah 29:10-14 foresees the exiles returning after seventy years of captivity in Babylon; Ezekiel 36:25-27 portrays God as cleansing the exiles and granting them a new heart so that they are empowered to obey God's ways.

The return of Jews from Babylonian exile after 538 BCE and the restoration of the post-exilic community did not live up to the expectations created by many of the prophetic promises. In the centuries that followed, political instability in Palestine and better economic prospects elsewhere encouraged many Jews to leave and seek a better life in locations across the Mediterranean world. Because of the limited nature of the post-exilic restoration and the increasing dispersion of the Jews, Judaism nurtured a sense of ongoing exile and longed for the time when God would fulfill the promises of restoration and return in most dramatic fashion.

NEW TESTAMENT REINTERPRETATION

During New Testament times, many Jews harbored intense hopes that God would fulfill the ancient prophecies by sending the Messiah to deliver them from foreign domination, return exiles to the land, and make of Israel a great nation. Hopes for national restoration were high on people's agenda; Jesus could not have avoided them. Jesus speaks extensively about the arrival of God's kingdom, something many Jews would have associated with the restoration of the Jewish people and the Jewish state. But for Jesus the kingdom has nothing to do with the creation of a state. God's kingdom is inaugurated by his ministry of healing, casting out demons, offering forgiveness to sinners, welcoming outcasts, feeding the hungry, preaching the good news, and calling for radical faithfulness to a new way of life.

Even the disciples harbored expectations of Israel's political restoration. Just before Jesus ascends to heaven they ask him,

"Lord, is this the time when you will restore the kingdom to Israel?" (Acts 1:6). Jesus responds with the promise of the Holy Spirit which will empower the disciples to proclaim the gospel to the ends of the earth (1:8). The kingdom of Jesus is not about a national state but rather about the great commission. It is about spreading the good news of God's kingdom and incorporating people from around the world into a new people of God whose lives will be oriented toward what God has accomplished and continues to accomplish through Jesus Christ.

Near the beginning of Luke's Gospel, the Holy Spirit inspires the priest Zachariah to praise God for the deliverance that Israel is about to experience. The language comes straight out of Old Testament promises of restoration. God has redeemed his people and raised up a savior from the house of David to save Israel from her enemies, all in fulfillment of Old Testament prophecy (1:67-79). The prophecies are being fulfilled, but nowhere in this hymn of praise, nor anywhere else in the New Testament, is there mention of God's salvation involving the creation of a Jewish state.

Hal Lindsey and others interpret Jesus' parable of the fig tree (Mark 13:28-31 and parallels in Matt. 24:32-35; Luke 21:29-33) as referring to the modern state of Israel. In the parable Jesus states that when the fig tree grows leaves, then we will know that summer—meaning his return—is near. Jesus' point is that since the fig is one of the last trees to produce leaves in the spring, the appearance of its leaves is a sign that summer is just around the corner. In a similar way, the fulfillment of the signs which Jesus has just described for his disciples will indicate that the end is near. Lindsey asserts that the fig tree represents Israel, viewing Israel's reemergence as a nation in 1948 as the "fig tree" putting forth its leaves, a sign of the imminent end.[3] The International Christian Embassy interprets the vague reference to destruction and salvation in Luke 21:23-24, 28 as a prediction by Jesus of the "scattering and latter-day regathering of the Jewish people"[4] and as evidence that Jesus clearly envisioned the restoration of the modern state of Israel.

If we interpret biblical texts this freely, then we can make them say pretty much whatever we want. Such over-interpretation is common in end-times scenarios. The fact that biblical passages about the end are often highly symbolic and use images and symbols no longer familiar to us encourages creative and even fanciful interpretations that often stray far from the actual content of the text.

One reason for such forced interpretations is that the New Testament never speaks of restoration of a Jewish state as being part of God's end-time plans. But since the state of Israel features so prominently in end-times scenarios, interpreters feel pressure to find references to it in the New Testament. One characteristic of end-times literature is a lack of consistency in methods of interpreting biblical texts. On the whole such interpreters insist on a literal reading of the Bible, as in the case of prophecies of Jewish return from exile. However, when it suits their purpose, they easily resort to symbolic interpretations that sometimes distort the plain meaning of a passage.

In the Old Testament, Israel, God, and the Promised Land form a triangle in God's scheme of salvation. Israel is a people under God, called to be separate from the nations of the world, living in the land promised by God. However, there are numerous Old Testament passages which envision a much broader community of God's people (Isa. 2:2-4; 25:6-8; 56:3-8). Christians believe that this dream of a non-nationalistic and multi-ethnic people of God finds fulfillment in the life of the church, even if quite imperfectly. Through the ministry of Christ the boundaries of God's chosen people are thrown wide open to welcome people from all lands and cultures.

The Old Testament promises of restoration belong to a period when God's focus is on one particular people living in a particular land. According to the New Testament, God's people are now found in communities gathered for worship, service, and faithful living across the globe. Therefore the New Testament offers a radical reinterpretation of the older promises of Israel's national restoration. The New Testament does not postpone the Old Testament promises of restoration; it transforms them.[5] Even before Jesus is born, Zechariah proclaims that the Old Testament promises of Jewish restoration will be fulfilled in the ministry of Jesus (Luke 1:68-79).

All four Gospel writers quote Isaiah 40:3 to describe John the Baptist's ministry of preparing for the salvation that is to come in Jesus (Matt. 3:3; Mark 1:2-3; Luke 3:4-6; John 1:23). The larger passage in Isaiah is about God's intervention to deliver Israel from exile (40:1-11). By quoting from this passage the Gospels signal that Jesus and the salvation he offers constitute fulfillment of God's promises to restore exiled Israel. When the disciples wish to know the timetable for Jewish national restoration, Jesus responds by giving them the great commission (Acts 1:6-8), indicating that the restoration of God's people occurs as the gospel is proclaimed.

Paul quotes two passages from Hosea about how God will restore Israel and renew his covenant with her after Israel has experienced destruction and exile (Rom. 9:25-26; see Hos. 1:10-11; 2:21-23). Hosea proclaims that a people once alienated from God will be restored and become God's precious people. According to Paul, these prophecies are fulfilled by the incorporation of Gentiles and Jews into the new people of God (9:24). Over and over the New Testament portrays the formation of the new people of God under the Lordship of Christ as representing the restoration of God's people foretold in the Old Testament.

End-times interpreters stray from the teaching of the New Testament by insisting that prophecies of Israel's restoration will be fulfilled literally, and that this fulfillment is postponed until just before the final arrival of God's kingdom. According to the New Testament, the old hopes for the renewal of God's people are being fulfilled through Christ and the community gathered around him. This is why the New Testament lays aside any expectations for restoration of a Jewish state, either in the first century or in the future.

Insisting on a literal interpretation of Old Testament promises of restoration gives end-time scenarios the appearance of being biblically grounded. However, such interpretations are not biblical enough in that they interpret Old Testament passages as if Jesus has not come, and as if Jesus, Paul, and the other New Testament writers have not provided guidance for how Christians ought to read and interpret prophetic promises in light of God's new act of salvation in Jesus Christ.[6]

THE ONGOING ROLE OF THE JEWISH PEOPLE

If the New Testament does not foresee a national restoration for the Jewish people, what role do the Jewish people continue to play in God's plans and purposes? On this issue different portions of Scripture express somewhat different perspectives. Paul is very positive about the ongoing role of the Jewish people in God's purposes. In Romans 3:1-4 he highlights the advantages of being Jewish, not least of which is having received God's special revelation. In chapter 11 he grapples with his lack of success in convincing Jews that Jesus is God's Messiah. He begins by asking if God has rejected his people. The immediate answer is a hearty "By no means!" (11:1) Why then will the Jews not accept God's salvation? The only answer Paul can give is that a temporary hardening of heart has come upon them, but he is convinced that in the end Israel will be saved (11:25-27). The bottom line is that God will never reject Israel as the chosen and beloved people (11:28-29).

Romans 11 uses the image of an olive tree to simultaneously stress two points: that Gentiles are becoming an integral part of God's people but the Jewish people continue to form the roots and trunk of this people (11:17-24). Far from being rejected by God or even being replaced by the church, the Jewish people continue to serve as the root and trunk which support the rest of the tree—that is, the church. Gentile believers are like shoots from a wild olive tree grafted into the Jewish people so these new believers may grow and bear fruit. Those Jews who have not accepted Jesus as the Messiah are likened to branches broken off the olive tree, but Paul is convinced that some day they will be regrafted onto the trunk (11:24).

Despite the special standing of the Jews, the bulk of Paul's ministry involved inviting Gentiles to accept God's salvation and become part of the new people of God. For Paul it was absolutely critical that the church of Christ overcome the barriers of race, ethnicity, class, and gender (Gal. 3:27-29). Ephesians 2 describes how Christ has broken down the dividing walls between Jews and Gentiles and created one new people of God (2:11-22).

In contrast to Paul's positive attitude, some New Testament passages suggest that God is rejecting the Jews. The parable of the wicked tenants who mistreat the vineyard owner's servants and kill his son stresses that the Jewish leaders have been so wicked and unfaithful that God will take the vineyard away from them and give it to others (Mark 12:1-12; Matt. 21:33-43; Luke 20:9-19). Vineyard is a common biblical image for Israel (see Isa. 5:1-7), so the parable accuses the Jewish leadership of being so totally evil that God will replace them with other leadership.

Technically, this parable is about the Jewish leaders and not the people as a whole, but many Jewish people respected and followed their leaders, and so the parable does in a sense speak of the rejection of both ordinary Jews and their leadership. According to the gospel of John, Jesus accuses the Jews of having the devil and not Abraham as their father (8:39-47), a rather strong rejection of their status as God's people. Hebrews 8:13 asserts that the new covenant sealed by Christ makes the older covenant of God with Israel obsolete and soon to pass away. The book of Acts closes with Paul in Rome observing how most of the Jews have rejected the salvation offered to them (28:23-28). He concludes that as a result God's salvation has been sent to the Gentiles because they will be more receptive.

The New Testament consistently claims for the church the promises and blessings granted to Israel in the Old Testament. The assumption behind this move is that God's promises and blessing are gifts to the people of God. God's act of salvation in Jesus Christ leads to the formation of the church, which now constitutes the new people of God. Therefore the church continues the story of God's people begun in the Old Testament, so the church can legitimately lay claim to the Scriptures and their promises. This does not mean that the church replaces Israel or that God rejects the Jewish people. Much of the early church retained a strong sense of both its connections and indebtedness to the Jewish people. After all, Jesus was Jewish, as were the first Christians and the entire first generation of leaders.

However, as the church became overwhelmingly Gentile, it did not take long for the church to both forget and denigrate its Jewish roots. Heated conflicts between Jews and Christians led to a less-than-amicable parting of ways, further contributing to negative sentiments toward Judaism. Eventually the church developed what is called replacement theology, asserting that the church has replaced Israel as God's chosen people. Drawing on New Testament texts like the ones mentioned above which are very critical of the Jews, the church began to claim that the Jewish people should be relegated to the dustbin of history. Instead of regarding the Jews as God's chosen people, the church demonized them as the arch-enemies of God because they had spurned the offer of salvation. Jews were called Christ-killers and even God-killers.

For nearly two thousand years the sin of anti-Judaism has been a blot on the church's life. In most countries of so-called Christian Europe, at various points in time Jews were subjected to persecution, forced conversions, large-scale expulsions, and even massacres. The Holocaust would probably never have occurred had centuries of Christian anti-Judaism not prepared the soil. As a church we have much for which to repent.

What then ought contemporary Christians to believe about the Jewish people? We can assert with Paul and the Old Testament that the Jews continue to be God's chosen people. Jews have kept faith with God for millennia, often under the most challenging circumstances. We should not claim that their covenant with God has been abrogated just because we believe that God has made a new covenant with us through Christ. What God's future plans and purposes are for the Jewish people is not ours to decide. The Bible provides us with little guidance on this question, so it is not an issue that need preoccupy us. Our agenda is to discern what it means for us to be faithful followers of Christ in the context in which we live.

While we can freely assert that the Jews continue to be God's chosen people, this does not mean that we need attach great theological significance to the state of Israel. The Jewish people and the state of Israel are not identical. The Jewish people survived for two thousand years without a state and may need to do so again in the future. Even today the majority of Jews in the world do not live in the state of Israel. We should acknowledge that many Jews hold the state of Israel close to their hearts, and for many its existence offers the promise and the comfort of a safe haven.

However, there is no need for Christians to pledge uncritical support for Israel because of convictions that Israel represents the fulfillment of Old Testament prophecy and is somehow essential to the unfolding of God's plans for the future. Israel is a state in the community of nations, all of whom are ultimately accountable to God. Therefore we ought to pray that Israel might pursue justice and righteousness in her national life, just like we pray the same for other nations. We can call on Israel to live up to internationally accepted standards of just behavior, just like we call on other nations to do the same. We should pray that God might shower Israel with blessings of peace, security, and prosperity, just like we pray that God's blessings might rain down on other nations and peoples as well.

QUESTIONS FOR DISCUSSION

1. What examples of anti-Judaism have you witnessed among Christians? What are some concrete ways in which the church can demonstrate its repentance of the sin of anti-Semitism?

2. What is your opinion of replacement theology? How can we as Christians affirm that through Christ we are the new people of God, and how can we claim the promises of the Old Testament, without at the same time nurturing negative attitudes toward the Jewish people?

3. How can we extend support to our Palestinian sisters and brothers in Christ, so that they do not feel like the Christian community in the West has abandoned or even turned against them?

SUGGESTIONS FOR ACTION

1. Pray for greater understanding between Jews and Christians. As part of the bridge-building process, commit yourself to better understanding the Jewish faith.

2. Pray for Palestinian Christians who feel alienated from their North American sisters and brothers in the faith who believe that Palestinians have no place in the land of Palestine.

NOTES

1. International Christian Embassy Jerusalem website, www.icej.g/about_min. Accessed Nov. 9, 2005.

2. John Hagee Ministries website, www.jhm.org/exos2.asp. Accessed Nov. 9, 2005.

3. Hal Lindsey, *The Late Great Planet Earth* (Grand Rapids: Zondervan, 1970), 53-54.

4. International Christian Embassy Jerusalem website, www.icej.org/abt/aut_doctrines. Accessed Nov. 9, 2005.

5. Colin Chapman, "Getting to the Point: Ten Questions for Christian Zionists," in *The Bible and the Land: An Encounter*, ed. Lisa Loden, Peter Walker, and Michael Wood (Jerusalem: Musalaha, 2000), 158.. The Chapman chapter can also be found in *The Land of Promise: Biblical, Theological and Contemporary Perspectives*, ed. Philip Johnston and Peter Walker (Downers Grove: InterVarsity, 2000), pp. 172-187.

6. For an insightful discussion of this matter see Chapman, "Getting to the Point," 158.

Palestinian Christians: The Forgotten Faithful

Timothy Seidel

For he is our peace; in his flesh he has made both groups into one and has broken down the dividing wall, that is, the hostility between us.
—Ephesians 2:14

On a pleasant Sunday afternoon in July 2000, members and pastors belonging to local Palestinian evangelical congregations from the Palestinian territories gathered at the Bethlehem Hotel to celebrate the formation of their council. An American woman present at the meeting approached one of the pastors and asked if she could say a few words to the assembly. The pastor, desiring to show courtesy to the guest, asked the emcee (also a Palestinian pastor) if the woman could say her few words.

The emcee, unaware of what was coming, agreed to let her talk. When the woman took the microphone, I couldn't believe the words that came out of her mouth. She professed to the Palestinian Evangelical Christians assembled there that she had a word from the Lord for them. "God," she said, wanted them "all to leave Israel and go to other Arab countries." She added that they must leave to make room for God's chosen people, the Jews. She warned the pastors and the audience that if they did not listen to the in-

structions which God had given her, God would pour his
wrath on them. When her agenda was recognized, one of
the pastors came and whisked her away from the pulpit,
but not before she served the whole assembly a mouthful of
what is known today as Christian Zionism.

This story, related by Alex Awad, the Palestinian pastor of
the East Jerusalem Baptist Church and dean of the Bethlehem
Bible College, poignantly reveals the extent to which some
Christian voices invalidate the concrete historical realities of
their Christian brothers and sisters living under occupation.
Such Christian Zionist voices not only ignore the realities of dispossession that have marked the experiences of both Christian
and Muslim Palestinians, past and present, but also go so far as
to justify violence, dispossession, and discrimination perpetrated against Palestinians.

Awad goes on to tell another story about a man he met in the
United States who, "after learning that I was a Palestinian Christian pastor, called to tell me that if I was truly a Bible-believing
Christian and a true follower of Jesus, I would know that God
has given the Holy Land to the Jews and that I and other Palestinian Christians should peacefully leave the country." Though
Awad does not believe that these two experiences represent fully
even the more Zionist persuasions of Christianity in America,
what it does reveal to him is that "many Christians in the United
States and around the world cling to these ideas without critically examining them."[1]

Stories like these reveal our need to be constantly vigilant
about how we read Scripture and how we do theology. We need
to ask basic questions about our identities, the agendas that we
bring to the text, and about who benefits from our reading and
interpretation, so we avoid violating others.

WHO IS "IN" AND WHO IS "OUT"?

When we talk about the "Christians in the Land," especially
Palestinian Christians, it is important to pay attention to our language of who is "in" and who is "out." As the story above indicates, some people may not see our Palestinian brothers and sisters as being in. From one perspective, Palestinians, be they
Christians or Muslims, are usurpers who should leave the land.

A reading of Scripture that erases Palestinians from the land is tantamount to a biblically justified ethnic cleansing of the Palestinian people. Mass dispossession and ethnic cleansing are universally condemned in contexts such as Rwanda, Sudan, or Bosnia. Christian Zionist readers of Scripture, however, implicitly (and sometimes explicitly) call for the removal of Palestinians from the land, a divinely mandated act of ethnic cleansing.

We must reflect biblically on the lines we draw marking who is in and who is out. If we take a look at the ministry of Jesus and the witness of the early church, for example, we see that all people are invited to become part of God's household. In the book of Ephesians, Gentiles are welcomed into "one new humanity" (2:15) because Christ has made peace between Jew and Gentile.

> So then, remember that at one time you Gentiles by birth, called "the uncircumcision" by those who are called "the circumcision"—a physical circumcision made in the flesh by human hands—remember that you were at that time without Christ, being aliens form the commonwealth of Israel, and strangers to the covenant of promise, having no hope and without God in the world. But now in Christ Jesus you who were once far off have been brought near by the blood of Christ. For he is our peace; in his flesh he has made both groups into one and has broken down the dividing wall, that is, the hostility between us. (Eph. 2:11-14)

The writer of Ephesians claims that Christ has become our peace. The vision of broken-down walls provides a striking contrast to the realities of concrete walls and barriers of separation in the land today.

In the book of Acts, meanwhile, we see Peter realizing that "God shows no partiality, but in every nation anyone who fears him and does what is right is acceptable to him" (10:34-35). And in Galatians, Paul reminds us that

> in Christ Jesus you are all children of God through faith. As many of you as were baptized into Christ have clothed yourselves with Christ. There is no longer Jew or Greek, there is no longer slave or free, there is no longer male and female; for all of you are one in Christ Jesus. And if you belong to Christ, then you are Abraham's offspring, heirs according to the promise. (Gal. 3:26-29)

Paul speaks beautifully of the mystery of this transforma-
tion, this vision of reconciliation. This sublime vision, however,
must be handled with great care. Especially when considered in
the context of centuries of Christian anti-Judaism, a life-giving
reading of Ephesians emphasizing Christian-Jewish reconciliation should not translate into a claim that the church, as a recon-
ciled body of Gentiles and Jews, has replaced the Jewish people.
Instead, we should be mindful of Paul's insistence in Romans 11
on God's abiding faithfulness to the people first called Israel. As
noted in the prior chapter, convinced that they have supplanted
the Jewish people, communities bearing the name of Christ have
too often adopted anti-Jewish attitudes—and worse, supported
anti-Jewish practices and policies. Reading Ephesians and the
Pauline corpus should not underwrite theologies that negate the
Jewish people but should instead correct our anti-Jewish ten-
dencies, pointing us toward Jesus and his call upon us and to the
mystery of God's continuing work through the Jewish people.

In Romans 11, Paul describes an organic relationship between Gentile and Jew, the relationship of a wild olive shoot
grafted in "to share the rich root of the olive tree" (11:17). Gentiles are grafted in. Israel is not replaced but supplemented. Paul
makes this point forcefully when he exhorts the reader not to
boast or grow arrogant because it is not the branches that support and provide sustenance for the tree or the roots but the root
that supports the entire tree (11:18). So instead of growing proud,
we are to "stand in awe" (11:20) at the works of God and understand our rightful role in God's plans, purposes, and activities in
history, noting both God's kindness and severity (11:22). It is
God and not we who grafts and removes, "for the gifts and the
calling of God are irrevocable" (11:30).

This mystery Paul speaks of is highlighted at the close of
chapter 11 in beautiful words of praise that remind readers of
their ignorance as to the ways of God (11:33-36):

> O the depth of the riches and wisdom and knowledge of
> God! How unsearcheable are his judgments and how in-
> scrutable his ways!
>   "For who has known the mind of the Lord?
>   Or who has been his counselor?"
>   "Or who has a given a gift to him to receive a gift in
>   return?"

For from him and through him and to him are all things. To
him be the glory forever. Amen.

God's gracious, mysterious purposes have been and are
being served through the calling of the Jewish people and the
church to live as embodied witnesses to God's redemptive purposes for humanity. We fail to do justice to the mysterious, un-
merited grace we received through Jesus if we exclude others—
Palestinians or Jews—from God's promises.

CHRISTIANITY IN PALESTINE

"You are a Christian?" a foreign tourist inquires with
marked disbelief of a Palestinian tour guide in Bethlehem.
"When did you convert?" Such unthinking and uninformed
comments are unfortunately common in Palestine-Israel. Even
in Bethlehem, this disbelief goes hand-in-hand with tourists' visits to the Church of the Nativity—visits in which tourists view
archaeological or religious sites as bearing witness to a time long
past without connection to the contemporary faith and reality of
the "living stones" who have continuously borne witness to the
gospel for two millennia.

Our ignorance as Christian visitors to this land carries with
it many assumptions and implications and perhaps reveals the
hidden racisms that continue to live deep inside us. We make assumptions as to who is central to the Christian world and who is
marginal. We have lost connection to the roots of our own faith
not just geographically but theologically. We have abandoned
solidarity with the "non-persons" of this world, with the "least
of these"—Christian or otherwise—those same persons with
whom Jesus is said to have explicitly identified himself (Matt.
25).

To think about our faith in the context of the Palestinian-Israeli conflict is to think about who is included. For Christians living in the United States and Canada, it is sometimes difficult to
think about the church as the new multi-ethnic, multi-racial people of God. Many Christians have a hard time seeing and relating to Christianity in the Arab world as living, vibrant communities of faith with rich spiritual and theological traditions. This
may be partly due to our lack of understanding about the shape
of Christianity in other parts of the world. It may also be partly

due to our often racist and ethnocentric notions of what a Christian should look like.

Christianity in the Arab world has had a long and lively history, including in Palestine. There one still finds today communities of faith that stretch back thousands of years to the very beginnings of the church, where Arabic is spoken in liturgies and sermons, and where the church has played an integral role in the development of society, whether in terms of providing leadership in very difficult times or in pioneering valuable social services like education.

Palestinian Christians belong to several traditional communities of faith, communities that can be grouped into four broad categories. The first are the traditions of the Eastern Orthodox churches. These would include the Greek Orthodox communities, claiming a continuous presence in the Holy Land since the times of the apostles.

The second group is made of up what are sometimes referred to as the "Oriental" Orthodox churches, such as the Syrian, Coptic, and Armenian Orthodox communities.[2]

A third category consists of those churches belonging to the Catholic family of churches. In addition to Roman Catholic communities, referred to in the Middle East as the "Latin" church, one finds "Eastern Catholic" or "Eastern Rite Catholic" churches. These churches, though in communion with Rome and recognizing the authority of the pope, have maintained their own distinctive liturgy and traditions. Members of such communities as Greek Catholic or Syrian Catholic outnumber the number of Latin Catholics in Palestine and have a long history of involvement in the Palestinian struggle for justice.

Finally, there are various Protestant communities. Among them are not only Anglican and Lutheran churches, present since the nineteenth century, but also independent evangelical churches, including Baptist, Pentecostal, and more.

Today of the roughly 3.8 million Palestinians living in the Occupied Territories, less than two percent are Christians. Of the 1.4 million Palestinians living inside Israel, meanwhile, roughly eight percent belong to Christian communities. Though small, these communities bear witness to two millennia of continuous Christian presence in the land called "holy" by much of the rest of the world.

THE CRISIS OF CHRISTIANITY IN PALESTINE

Christianity in Palestine-Israel today is experiencing what many describe as a crisis. This crisis is not due to the growth of so-called Islamic fundamentalism or the persecution of "believers" by their Muslim neighbors, misrepresentations used to distract from the realities of military occupation. Instead, the plight of the Palestinian Christian is very much connected to that of the Palestinian Muslim in that both, whether in the Occupied Territories or inside Israel itself, are experiencing daily injustices in the form of oppressive policies imposed on them by the Israeli government.

Like their Muslim neighbors, who are prevented by checkpoints and roadblocks from making pilgrimage to the Al-Aqsa Mosque in Jerusalem, Christians in the West Bank and the Gaza Strip are denied basic religious freedoms, routinely prohibited from traveling very short distances to worship in one of the most holy sites in Christianity—the Church of the Holy Sepulcher in the Old City of Jerusalem, where the church commemorates Jesus' crucifixion, burial, and resurrection from the dead.

Palestinian Christians, like their Muslim brothers and sisters, have experienced a long history of dispossession and have not been immune to Israeli policies of occupation and discrimination. If anything, they have felt more strongly the feelings of forsakenness, knowing full well that many Christians in North America and Europe support without question the state of Israel in its oppression of their people.

Meanwhile, daily experiences of humiliation at checkpoints, of land confiscation to make way for the separation barrier, the illegal occupation and colonization of Palestinian territory, lack of mobility and access to basic services, unemployment, poverty, and no sense of hope for a better future for their children all contribute to a growing emigration of Palestinian Christians from the historical land of Palestine.

For the Palestinian Christians of Bethlehem, for example, traveling the six mile (ten km) distance to Jerusalem's Old City is impossible without special permission. Roughly half of Bethlehem's residents are Christian. Church leaders estimate that over 2,000 Christians have emigrated from the Bethlehem area since September 2000, representing a decline of more than nine percent of Bethlehem's total Christian population.[3]

Alex Awad reminds us that "Palestinian Christians have ex-
isted in the Holy Land since the day of Pentecost and have kept
the torch of Christianity burning faithfully for the past two thousand years." The erosion of Christianity in her birthplace, he
poignantly observes "is a loss for the body of Christ everywhere.
Can we imagine the Holy Land devoid of the Christian presence
and a church which has been a faithful witness for Christ since
the day the church was born?"[4]

FORSAKENNESS AND HOPE

Cedar Duaybis, a Palestinian Christian laywoman who
serves on the board of the Sabeel Ecumenical Liberation Theology Center in Jerusalem, tells of making a presentation to an
adult Bible study in the United States. As she described the situation for Palestinian Christians under Israeli occupation, one individual vehemently objected that "Israel is Christian!" For Duaybis, the assertion that "Israel is Christian" encapsulated how
many Christians place unconditional support of the state of Israel against the right of Palestinian Christians and Muslims to
live securely "under vine and fig tree" (Mic. 4:4).

Having such encounters leave Duaybis and other Palestinian Christians feeling forsaken by the rest of the Christian world.
Duaybis fears that the feeling of forsakenness experienced by
these "living stones" who bear witness to two thousand years of
Christianity in the "Holy Land" will only contribute to further
emigration, leaving behind only historical markers, or "dead
stones," to tell the story of these communities.

Struggling with the tensions of feeling forsaken while seeking a critical hope is a great challenge. Despair in the Holy Land
is very real, and learning how to talk about God amid such pain
requires recognizing that the starting point of any relevant theological reflection must begin with the question "My God, why
have you forsaken us?" For Western Christians concerned with
justice, peace, and reconciliation in Palestine-Israel, discovering
our role as one of listening to the cries of despair seriously while
being a witness to critical hope begins with seeing our inextrica-
ble connectedness—it begins with us not forsaking each other.

As Christians who come from a privileged part of the world,
our convictions should compel us to listen to the voices of our

Palestinian brothers and sisters, voices too often silenced. As we learn from Jesus' experience of "God-forsakenness," we should also learn from Palestinians who share their lives with us—their despair and their hopes—what it means to participate in God's reign of peace and justice.

QUESTIONS FOR DISCUSSION

1. Both Israelis and Palestinians—Jews, Muslims, and Christians—have strong attachments to Jerusalem: spiritual, social, economic, and political. The separation barrier, however, is separating Palestinians in Jerusalem from Palestinians outside of Jerusalem and in some cases is dividing Palestinian neighborhoods of Jerusalem from each other. Palestinian Christians and Muslims in the West Bank can rarely visit their holy sites in Jerusalem. Can such a wall make for peace? How would you feel if you were prohibited from practicing your religion freely?

2. What media reports (radio, newspaper, television, other) have you heard recently that mentioned Palestinian Christians? What was reported?

SUGGESTIONS FOR ACTION

1. View the MCC video *Walking the Path Jesus Walked* with your church or with some friends to learn more about the Christian presence in Palestine-Israel and the larger Arab world (available from your local MCC office or online at www.mcc.org/catalog).

2. Attend worship services in an Orthodox church. Reflect on the way in which this worship engages your senses. How is it similar to worship in your own church? How is it different?

3. Read Father Elias Chacour's *Blood Brothers* and *We Belong to the Land* for insight into the Palestinian Christian experience.

4. Contact the MCC Washington, D.C. office (www.mcc.org/us/washington), MCC's office in Ottawa (www.mcc.org/canada/ottawa), or the Sabeel Ecumenical Liberation Theology Center (www.sabeel.org), to learn more about how to work toward justice and peace in a way that will make Palestinian Christians feel less forsaken by their brothers and sisters in North America.

NOTES

1. In "Christian Zionism and Peace in the Holy Land," *MCC Peace Office Newsletter* 35/3 (July-September 2005).

2. The "Oriental" Orthodox churches are distinguished historically from other Orthodox traditions by their rejection of the decisions reached at the fourth ecumenical council in Chalcedon in 451 CE. Syrian, Coptic, and Armenian Orthodox churches are also sometimes referred to as "Non-Chalcedonian" as opposed to the "Chalcedonian" identity of other Eastern Orthodox communities.

3. For more on current conditions in Bethlehem, see the report from the Office for the Coordination of Humanitarian Affairs (OCHA) and the Office of the Special Coordinator for the Peace Process in the Middle East (UNSCO), "Costs of Conflict: The Changing Face of Bethlehem" (December 2004).

4. In "Christian Zionism and Peace in the Holy Land," *MCC Peace Office Newsletter* 35/3 (July-September 2005).

Chapter 12

Signs of the Kingdom in the Land

Christi Hoover Seidel

When Jesus saw the crowds, he went up the mountain; and after he sat down, his disciples came to him. Then he began to speak, and taught them, saying: "Blessed are the poor in spirit, for theirs is the kingdom of heaven.

"Blessed are those who mourn, for they will be comforted.

"Blessed are the meek, for they will inherit the earth.

"Blessed are those who hunger and thirst for righteousness, for they will be filled.

"Blessed are the merciful, for they will receive mercy.

"Blessed are the pure in heart, for they will see God.

"Blessed are the peacemakers, for they will be called children of God.

"Blessed are those who are persecuted for righteousness' sake, for theirs is the kingdom of heaven."

—Matthew 5:1-10

THEN AND NOW

Many pilgrims who come to the Holy Land make their way to Galilee and visit the Church of the Beatitudes overlooking the Sea of Galilee, a place to remember Jesus' Sermon on the Mount.

Amid the beautiful, calm scenery—the luscious greenness of the mountainside covered with trees, the array of flowers and the hint of a slight breeze—one can easily feel far removed from the devastating effects of the conflict in this land. Drive south for thirty minutes or so, however, and one quickly reaches the first military checkpoint, a sign that one has entered the occupied West Bank; the promise and comfort of the Beatitudes begin to feel sadly distant.

Many times, in our conversations with Palestinians, we hear the phrase, *Wayn Allah? Where is God?* Palestine is a place where people, especially our Christian brothers and sisters, feel forsaken. Forsaken by Christians, by the church around the world; sometimes forsaken by God.

Here it is easy to despair and difficult to hope. Yet, from those who are suffering most, I find reason to hope. Through them I am reminded that Jesus was not unfamiliar with the suffering of people around him. His sermons, his teachings, and his life were for "the least of these." Jesus embodied hope for these "least"—and for us. Living amid despair, he did not succumb to it. Rather, his death and resurrection absorbed and defeated despair, giving us reason to hope.

GOD'S KINGDOM: A CALL TO ACTION

My own understanding of the promise of the Beatitudes began to broaden when I read the biographical reflections of Elias Chacour, a Palestinian Melkite (Greek Catholic) priest (now bishop) from the Galilee. Chacour, whose ancestral village of Kfar Bir'im was destroyed by the Israeli military shortly after the war of 1948, looks to Jesus' mother tongue of Aramaic to understand the message of the Beatitudes today. "We are accustomed," Chacour notes,

> to hearing the Beatitudes expressed passively. "Blessed" is the translation of the world *makarioi,* used in the Greek New Testament. However, when I look further back to Jesus' Aramaic, I find that the original word was *ashray,* from the verb *yahar.* Ashray does not have this passive quality to it at all. Instead, it means "to set yourself on the right way for the right goal; to turn around, repent; to become straight or righteous." . . . When I understand Jesus'

words in the Aramaic, I translate like this:
Get up, go ahead, do something, move, you
   who are hungry
and thirsty for justice, for you shall be satisfied.
Get up, go ahead, do something, move, you peacemakers,
for you shall be called children of God.[1]

Read this way, the focus in the Beatitudes shifts from future fulfillment to current action. Jesus' proclamation of the kingdom, moreover, directs our attention to the present. "Repent," Jesus calls, "for the kingdom of heaven has come near" (Matt. 4:17). Jesus brought God's kingdom to us. Later, when he is teaching the disciples to pray, he instructs them to ask for God's reign to break into the present moment: "Your kingdom come, Your will be done, on earth as it is in heaven" (Matt. 6:10). When asked by the Pharisees regarding the coming of the kingdom, Jesus replies, "nor will they say, 'Look, here it is!' or 'There it is!' For, in fact, the kingdom of God is among you" (Luke 17:21). God's kingdom is here now.

What does God's reign look like? In his letter to the church at Rome, Paul declares, "For the kingdom of God is not food and drink but righteousness and peace and joy in the Holy Spirit" (Rom. 14:17). Paul stresses that divisions about table fellowship should not deter the Christian pursuit of peace and right relationships. For Paul, it is more important for Christians to focus on the unity and love that Christ's life, death, and resurrection bring us, rather than on matters that divide. The kingdom as described by Paul is inclusive, driven by love and forgiveness. God's reign means the establishment of justice and peace for all of humanity. Because Christ lived, died, and was resurrected, we know that the power of death has lost its sting and cannot, therefore, be the final word on how history plays itself out.

LIGHTS IN THE DARKNESS

Living in a place in which suffering, oppression, and despair are just outside my front doorstep, I have been challenged to reexamine what the kingdom of God means and to find an answer to that desperate question, "Where is God?"

All I had to do, I began to realize, was to look around me, to take closer note of the Palestinians and Israelis with whom I live and work. Looking more carefully at these people, I began to see the kingdom of God being lived out even in the darkest of places.

Blessed are the poor in spirit, for theirs is the kingdom of heaven— Palestinian Christians continue to worship in Bethlehem in the face of occupation and distress.

Luke 2:15 says, "'Let us go now to Bethlehem and see this thing that has taken place. . . .'" Bethlehem is currently being surrounded by a wall nearly thirty feet (ca. nine meters) high and a network of electronically monitored fences, barbed wire, trenches, and patrol roads. A new and bigger checkpoint has been set in place between the ghetto Bethlehem is becoming and its closest and most important neighboring city, Jerusalem.

Most of the residents of the Bethlehem district (around half of whom are Christian) have thus been cut off from Jerusalem.[2] While pilgrims from around the world visit the churches on the Mt. of Olives and in Jerusalem's Old City, Bethlehemites cannot travel the few kilometers to pray at the church where tradition says Jesus was crucified, buried, and resurrected. Palestinian Christians and Muslims alike are denied access to the social, cultural, and medical institutions in Jerusalem. Meanwhile, unemployment and poverty continue to rise as job opportunities disappear, thanks to the severe restrictions on movement posed by the separation barrier and the checkpoints around Bethlehem. As Palestinians, both Christian and Muslim, look to emigrate to other countries in search of employment, the Christian population in the birthplace of Christianity declines.

Church bells, however, still ring in Bethlehem. The remaining Christians still attend services, worship their creator, offer prayers of thanksgiving, and are challenged by sermons of hope. These Christians still light candles in the churches as a testimony of their faith and as a witness of their continued presence in their homeland. They inspire other Christians with their dedication, with their *sumud*, or steadfastness. *Theirs is the kingdom of heaven.*

Blessed are those who mourn, for they shall be comforted. Bereaved Israeli and Palestinian parents make up the Families Forum, a group that gathers to share and heal mutual pain.

More than 300 mourning family members take part in the Families Forum of the Parents' Circle, an initiative of Palestinians and Israelis joined by their grief over the death of a family member due to the violence of the Palestinian-Israeli conflict.

The forum is dedicated to preventing further bereavement. Members agree that there should be an end to occupation and a reconciliation born of "mutual consideration and respect of each others' national and legitimate aspirations." They act to educate the public and to influence policy makers. They raise awareness that while bereavement can be used to deepen the hostility between Palestinians and Israelis, it can also be a time when people draw closer together in grief. *They will be comforted.*

Blessed are the meek, for they will inherit the earth—Palestinians plant olive trees where they have been uprooted.

The East Jerusalem YMCA Olive Tree Campaign, Keep Hope Alive, began in response to the confiscation of thousands of acres of farmland and the uprooting and destruction of thousands of olive trees for the construction of the separation barrier. With this devastation threatening the economic future for Palestinian farming families, planting trees has become a nonviolent means of resisting occupation and of proclaiming one's hope in a better future. The East Jerusalem YMCA, a Palestinian Christian social-service agency with projects throughout the Occupied Territories, calls on Christians world-wide to participate in this campaign of hope. *They will inherit the earth.*

Blessed are those who hunger and thirst for righteousness, for they will be filled—Rabbis seek to be the voice of conscience in Israel.

The psalmist proclaims that those who keep God's judgments and practice righteousness at all times will be blessed (Ps. 119:172). Rabbis for Human Rights, an Israeli organization dedicated to giving voice to the Jewish tradition of human rights, takes this proclamation as the foundation for its work. Not only does Rabbis for Human Rights work for justice for the economically and socially marginalized inside Israel—such as foreign workers, women, Ethiopian Jews, and persons lacking adequate health care—it also speaks and acts against the human rights violations against Palestinians in the Occupied Territories and inside Israel.

The director of Rabbis for Human Rights, Arik Ascherman, has been arrested numerous times while attempting to prevent the bulldozing of Palestinian homes. Rabbi Ascherman and his colleagues work for a future in which both Israelis and Palestinians will sit secure under vine and fig tree, with no one to make them afraid. *They will be filled.*

Blessed are the merciful, for they shall receive mercy—Israelis help rebuild demolished Palestinian homes.

The Israeli Committee Against House Demolitions (ICAHD) is a network of Israelis committed to nonviolence that stands against the destruction of Palestinian homes. Over the past decades the Israeli military has demolished thousands of Palestinian homes, sometimes as collective punishment, sometimes on the pretext of "security measures," and sometimes because homes had been built without permits from the Israeli military government in the Occupied Territories. ICAHD calls attention to discriminatory zoning practices that prevent Palestinians from building on their land while Israeli settlers build at will, organizes nonviolent actions to protect homes slated for demolition, and seeks to explain to the Israeli public that policies of house demolitions poison the possibilities for future Palestinian-Israeli peace.

Working alongside Palestinians, ICAHD organizes summer camps to rebuild homes destroyed according to Israeli military orders. Persons from around the world join in these summer rebuilding camps. Those who could easily benefit from lives of privilege and power decide instead to be catalysts for change in their societies and world, joining in cooperative effort those persons marginalized from the centers of power. *They shall receive mercy.*

Blessed are the pure in heart, for they will see God—Innocent children suffer from the conflicts of older generations.

Christine Sa'adeh was just ten years old when she was killed by Israeli soldiers inside her hometown of Bethlehem on March 25, 2003. Christine was riding with her father and sister when their car came under fire because it matched the description of a car being driven by wanted Palestinian men. All of the bullets that hit Christine's father and sister first passed through her body, shielding them from death. Christine's father and sister were hospitalized for several days, leaving her mother to grieve alone at her funeral. Christine's death was devastating and traumatic for her young friends, yet they lifted up their suffering voices and the life of Christine in their writings in a book aptly entitled, *The Wall Cannot Stop Our Stories*.[3] *They will see God.*

Blessed are the peacemakers, for they will be called children of God—Palestinians work to maintain peaceful relations within their own society and to train and educate youth to make a positive impact in their society and beyond.

Wi'am means "cordial relationships" in Arabic. Since the Israeli occupation has interrupted the traditional ways of life among groups in Palestinian society and has forced many Palestinians in rural areas to move into towns, as land is being confiscated, the result is that Palestinian society experiences many new and intense internal stresses. The Wi'am Palestinian Conflict Resolution Center has been working for over a decade to respond to the needs of the local community, resolving conflicts with traditional and Western methods of conflict resolution. *They will be called children of God.*

Blessed are those who are persecuted for righteousness' sake, for theirs is the kingdom of heaven—Ordinary Israeli citizens work to educate themselves and their society about the tragedy of the *Nakba*, or the catastrophe of 1948.

The Zochrot Association is an Israeli organization dedicated to educating the Israeli public about the Nakba or catastrophe of 1948, when upwards of 500 Palestinian villages were destroyed by Israeli military forces. Zochrot, which means remembering in Hebrew, draws volunteers from among educational activists who seek to uncover those histories too often erased by dominant narratives. These inspiring workers have been arrested and have received death threats just for posting signs in Hebrew and Arabic at sites of destroyed Palestinian villages inside what is now Israel. The signs bear village street names from before 1948 and identify ruins of churches, mosques, and private homes that remain as mute testimonies to a violently suppressed past.

Zochrot members believe that acknowledging Israel's past actions is the first step in taking responsibility for that past and its ongoing repercussions. They also believe in equal rights for all people of the region, including the rights of Palestinian refugees to return to their homes. *Theirs is the kingdom of heaven.*

A KINGDOM ALIVE

Just as a person's eyesight takes awhile to adjust in darkness to be able to see, it wasn't until I began to focus on these lights that I was able to see hope amid a desperate situation. I realized that there were many lights flickering. What I had to do was to open my eyes and see them. Of course, that doesn't mean that I don't see or feel the darkness. At times it is overwhelming. Often, it is tempting to close my eyes in despair at the horror that infiltrates a place like this. But that's not what those around me are doing, those for whom Palestine-Israel is their permanent home. Many Palestinians and Israelis do not have the ability to walk away, and many of those who do have decided to stay.

But darkness doesn't just exist in Palestine-Israel or only in places of despair and hopelessness—darkness exists every-where. Living in the light of the Beatitudes is the challenge for Christians in any area of darkness. This is the kingdom of God among us. I soon realized the power of the old Chinese proverb, "It's better to light a candle than to curse the darkness." For me, it came down to a choice—what did I choose for my life? If I spent my time cursing the darkness, I'd be left with a life full of curses. If I spent my time lighting candles, little-by-little the light would strengthen and I would see the darkness being illumi-nated by the cumulative effect of small efforts.

I have decided I want my life to be dictated by hope and not curses. As a Mennonite peace worker in Palestine-Israel, I have been blessed by the embodied testimonies of hope of many Palestinians and Israelis. Through their lives and efforts, God is pointing toward a future of peace, justice, and reconciliation in the land. Though their efforts may at times seem small in com-parison to the powers of violence and dispossession, these peacemakers faithfully live out the biblical vision of God's peo-ple—both Israeli and Palestinian—dwelling securely in the land.

"The light shines in the darkness, and the darkness did not overcome it"(John 1:5).

DISCUSSION QUESTIONS

1. What are your thoughts on the perspective that Elias Cha-cour brings to the Beatitudes?

2. What are some of the ways Jesus tries to express the king-dom of God through parables in the Gospels? How do these parables describe a reign of justice and peace here on earth?

3. How can the various examples of "Lights in the Darkness" be inspirations for us to live in the light of the Beatitudes in the dark areas around us?

SUGGESTIONS FOR ACTION

1. Visit the websites of the groups highlighted in this chapter and find ways that you can be involved in the work of God's kingdom in Palestine-Israel.

2. Bring a group to visit the region to see the situation first-hand and to meet people who are working for peace and justice.

3. Have your Sunday school group plan a "Palestine-Israel Sunday" at your church. Highlight the work of Palestinians and Israelis working for justice, peace, and reconciliation.

4. Pray for the groups discussed in this chapter, asking that their commitment to justice, peace, and reconciliation might serve as an inspiration to other Palestinians and Israelis.

NOTES

1. Elias Chacour, *We Belong to the Land: The Story of a Palestinian Is-raeli who Lives for Peace and Reconciliation* (New York: HarperCollins, 1990), 143-144.

2. *O Little Town of Bethlehem: What Is Its Future?* (Bethlehem: Applied Reseach Institute-Jerusalem and International Center of Bethlehem, 2005), 21.

3. *The Wall Cannot Stop Our Stories: Diaries from Palestine 2000-2004* (Bethlehem: Terra Sancta School for Girls, Sisters of St. Joseph, Bethle-hem, 2004), 224-244.

Timeline of the Palestinian-Israeli Conflict

1516-1918

> Palestine is a part of southern Greater Syria under Ottoman rule; Ottoman Empire controls most of the Middle East

1880s Beginning of Arab movement for independence from the Ottoman Empire; first wave (*aliyah*) of Zionist immigration to Palestine

1896-1897

> Publication of Theodor Herzl's *The Jewish State* sets the stage for political Zionism; first World Zionist Congress meets in Basel, Switzerland and discusses establishment of a Jewish state

1914-1918

> World War I; Britain makes conflicting commitments regarding future of Palestine in the Husayn-McMahon correspondence (1915-1916), Sykes-Picot Agreement (1916), and Balfour Declaration (1917); end of Ottoman Empire

1919-1920

> U.S.-sponsored King-Crane Commission reports of Arab desires for independence; newly created League of Nations ignores King-Crane and divides Arab lands into entities called mandates, intended to create nation-states for the indigenous people; Britain accepts mandate for Palestine; clashes between Palestinians and Jews in Palestine

1929 *Al-Buraq*/Western Wall riots result in violent clashes between Palestinians and Zionists

1933-1935
Hitler comes to power in Germany; Germany's Nuremberg Laws formalize discrimination against Jews; Jewish migration into Palestine increases

1936-1939
Arab Revolt in Palestine; with the assistance of Zionist militias, Britain crushes rebellion, expels or executes its leaders; ever-increasing persecution of Jews in Germany

1937 British Peel Commission report proposes the partition of Palestine into Jewish and Arab areas

1939 British MacDonald White Paper recommends restrictions on Jewish immigration and land purchases and calls for establishment within ten years of independent, binational state in Palestine, angering Jews and ending British-Zionist alliance

1940s
World War II in Europe; Holocaust: Nazi regime responsible for death of approximately six million Jews (the *Shoah*); Lebanon becomes independent in 1943; Syria in 1944; Jordan in 1946

1945 United Nations (UN) established; World War II ends, leaving 100,000 Eastern and Central European Jews in "displaced persons" camps

1946 Anglo-American Commission of Inquiry recommends UN trusteeship over Palestine; Palestinian and Jewish violence against British and each other

1947 Britain requests UN deal with the question of Palestine; UN General Assembly Resolution 181 calls for Palestine to be divided into a Jewish state (fifty-six percent of Palestine), an Arab state (forty-three percent of Palestine), with an internationally controlled *corpus separatum* for Bethlehem and for Jerusalem

1948 Britain ends its mandate, Israel declares independence, and Arab states declare war against Israel; Israel gains control of seventy-seven percent of British Mandatory Palestine, including some areas designated for Palestinian Arab state; Jordan and Egypt hold the West Bank and the Gaza Strip respectively, Jerusalem divided; 750,000-900,000 Palestinians displaced before, during, and after the fighting are not allowed to return; UN General Assembly Resolution 194 supports right of Palestinian refugees to regain their homes if they so desire or to receive compensation if they choose not to return; 150,000 Palestinians remain in new state of Israel

1949 Armistice between Israel and Arab states

1950 Israel passes the Law of Return, guaranteeing the right of every Jew in the world to settle in Israel, and the Absentee Property Law, leading to extensive confiscation of Palestinian property

1956-1957
Suez War begins when Israel, supported by Britain and France, attacks Egypt; Israel conquers, and later withdraws from, Sinai and the Gaza Strip under threat of economic sanctions by U.S. President Eisenhower

1964 Palestine Liberation Organization (PLO) is established

1966 Fatah (founded in 1959 by Yasser Arafat and others) conducts first guerrilla action against Israel

1967 June (Six-Day) War begins when Israel attacks Egypt, claiming it is acting preemptively; Israel occupies West Bank, Gaza Strip, Egyptian Sinai, and Syrian Golan Heights, expands Jerusalem boundaries, extends Israeli law over East Jerusalem, and places rest of Occupied Territories under military administration; 400,000 Palestinians become refugees; UN Security Council Resolution 242 calls for withdrawal of Israeli troops from territories newly occupied; PLO becomes umbrella organization for various Palestinian resistance groups and adopts national charter

1968-1969
Israel begins to establish Jewish settlements in newly occupied territories in violation of the Fourth Geneva Convention; PLO adopts goal of a democratic secular state in all of Mandate Palestine; Arafat named chairman of PLO

1968-1970
War of Attrition between Israel and Egypt, Israel and Syria

1970 PLO expelled from Jordan and moves to Lebanon

1973 October (Yom Kippur/Ramadan) War begins when Egypt seeks to regain by force Egyptian land that Israel captured in 1967; UN Security Council Resolution 338 calls for ceasefire and comprehensive peace conference; oil embargo by Arab petroleum-exporting countries

1974 Arab League declares PLO the sole legitimate representative of Palestinian people; Arafat addresses UN, which grants PLO observer status in 1975

1977 Likud wins Israeli elections and Menachem Begin becomes prime minister; colonization of Occupied Territories increases; Egyptian President Anwar Sadat visits Jerusalem and addresses the Israeli Knesset; peace negotiations begin between Israel and Egypt

1978 Begin, Sadat, and U.S. President Jimmy Carter sign the Camp David Accords; the Sinai returned to Egypt in exchange for recognition of Israel; sets framework for settling Israeli-Palestinian conflict; Israel invades Lebanon, occupies its southern border.

1979 Begin and Sadat sign Israeli-Egyptian peace treaty in Washington

1980 Israel's Basic Law on Jerusalem annexes East Jerusalem, declares Jerusalem its eternal, undivided capital; UN Security Council condemns action

1981 Israel attacks Iraqi nuclear reactor; U.S. sponsors ceasefire between Israel and the PLO that lasts until June 1982; Israel annexes Syrian Golan Heights

1982 Israeli invasion of Lebanon; PLO evacuated from Beirut to Tunis; U.S. President Reagan presents peace plan; Phalangist massacre at Sabra and Shatila refugee camps near Beirut; 400,000 Israelis demonstrate and call for investigation of Israel's role in massacre

1985 Israel withdraws from most of Lebanon, leaving an Israeli-allied Lebanese force in control of the southern areas; Israel bombs Tunisian headquarters of the PLO

1987-1993

Predominantly nonviolent (demonstrations, strikes, tax resistance) Palestinian *intifada*, a Palestinian popular uprising in the Occupied Territories

1988 Palestinian National Council (PNC) accepts UN Security Council resolutions 242 and 338, recognizing the state of Israel, and declares the state of Palestine at a meeting in Algiers; Arafat condemns terrorism; U.S. opens direct discussions with PLO

1991 U.S.-led coalition attacks Iraq, after it invaded Kuwait in 1990; international Arab-Israeli peace conference in Madrid with Palestinians included in joint Jordanian-Palestinian delegation

1992 Ongoing bilateral and multilateral peace talks; Yitzhak Rabin becomes Israeli prime minister; U.S. Bush administration attempts to limit Israeli settlement by delaying loan guarantees

1993 Israel drastically restricts Palestinian movement between Israel and the Occupied Territories; Israel and the PLO sign Declaration of Principles (the Oslo Accords) on interim self-government arrangements

1994 Massacre of Palestinians praying in Hebron mosque by Israeli settler Baruch Goldstein; Arafat establishes Palestinian Authority (PA) headquarters in Gaza; Israel and Jordan sign peace treaty; Rabin, Peres, Arafat receive Nobel Peace Prize.

1995 Oslo II Accords establish three types of control in the West Bank (Area A: direct Palestinian control, Area B: Palestinian civilian control and Israeli security control, Area C: Israeli control); Rabin assassinated in Tel Aviv

1996 First Palestinian elections for president and parliament result in Arafat victory; Palestinian suicide bombings in Jerusalem and Tel Aviv; Benjamin Netanyahu elected Israeli prime minister

1997 Hebron Protocol divides West Bank city of Hebron into Israeli and Palestinian areas; Israel begins building Har Homa settlement between East Jerusalem and Bethlehem resulting in widespread international protests; peace process frozen; closures imposed in West Bank and Gaza

1998 PLO renounces anti-Israel clauses in PLO charter

1999 Ehud Barak elected Israeli prime minister; final status talks begin

2000 Palestinian Authority has direct or indirect control of 40 percent of the West Bank and 65 percent of Gaza; U.S. President Clinton-led Camp David II summit and negotiations end in failure; new Palestinian uprising, or *al-Aqsa intifada*, begins, sparked by Ariel Sharon's visit to *al-Haram al-Sharif*/Temple Mount with 1,000 armed guards

2001 Renewed Palestinian-Israeli negotiations at Taba fail; Palestinian hard-liners continue suicide bombings against Israeli military and civilians; Israeli forces increase "targeted killings" (assassinations) of Palestinians and armed incursions into Palestinian-controlled areas; Sharon elected Israeli prime minister; U.S. Mitchell Report calls for immediate ceasefire and complete freeze on building of Jewish settlements in the West Bank and Gaza Strip

2002 Israel forcefully reoccupies nearly all Palestinian areas evacuated as part of Oslo process; Arafat under house arrest in Ramallah; Arab League endorses Saudi peace plan to recognize Israel in exchange for end of occupation; Israel begins construction of "separation barrier" within the West Bank, confiscating additional Palestinian lands; "The Quartet" (European Union, Russia, U.S., UN) proposes "road map" to peace

2003 U.S.-initiated war against Iraq overthrows Saddam Hussein and occupation of Iraq begins; Mahmoud Abbas (Abu Mazen) chosen as Palestinian prime minister and later replaced by Ahmed Qurei; Israel completes first stage of separation barrier despite international opposition

2004 Sharon announces unilateral Gaza withdrawal plan and gains U.S. support; Palestinian Authority President Yasser Arafat dies; International Court of Justice rules that the route of Israel's separation barrier violates international law

2005 Mahmoud Abbas elected President of the Palestinian Authority; Sharm el-Sheikh summit results in a cease-fire by militant groups; in State of the Union address U.S. President Bush recommits to two-state solution and asks Congress for additional aid to the Palestinians; Gaza "disengagement" is completed in September

2006 Israeli Prime Minister Sharon suffers a serious stroke; Deputy Prime Minister Ehud Olmert assumes power, becomes prime minister, and announces "convergence" plan to unilaterally declare Israel's borders by 2010 by annexing major settlement blocs and the Jordan Valley, leaving isolated islands of land on 40-50 percent of the West Bank for a future Palestinian "state"; Hamas wins majority in the Palestinian Legislative Council elections and the international community imposes a devastating boycott on the PA; following the abduction of Israeli soldiers, Israel launches major military campaigns against Lebanon and Gaza

2007 The Mecca agreement is signed between Fatah and Hamas forming a Palestinian national unity government

Adapted from timelines found at the Middle East Research and Information Project website (www.merip.org/palestine-israel_primer/ MERIP-I-P-timeline11-06-03.html), the Churches for Middle East Peace website (www.cmep.org/documents/Timeline.htm), and from *Ilan Pappé, A History of Modern Palestine: One Land, Two Peoples* (Cambridge: Cambridge University Press, 2004).

Glossary of Terms

Absentee Property Law: Israeli law adopted in March 1950, classifying anyone who was a citizen or resident of one of the Arab states or a Palestinian citizen on November 29, 1947, but had left his or her place of residence, even to take refuge elsewhere within Palestine, as an "absentee." Absentee property was turned over to the "Custodian of Absentee Property" who then sold it to the Israeli Development Authority, empowered by the Knesset, Israel's parliament. This action provided a veneer of legality to the dispossession of a million Palestinians.

Ashkenazi: (Old Hebrew for a German) Reference to Jews of Eastern European descent.

Balfour Declaration: Letter sent on November 2, 1917, by British Foreign Secretary Arthur James Balfour to Baron de Rothschild pledging British support for the establishment of a Jewish "national home" in Palestine.

British Mandate: After World War I, the Arab lands of the defeated and dissolved Ottoman Empire were divided into territories called mandates that were eventually to become nation-states for the indigenous people. Britain accepted the mandate for Palestine in 1922, and with it the responsibility eventually to turn the country over to self-rule, despite having made conflicting agreements with Arab leadership (the Husayn-McMahon correspondence, 1915-1916), the French (Sykes-Picot Agreement, 1916), and European Zionists (Balfour Declaration, 1917). Britain ended its mandate in May 1948.

Checkpoint: Roadblocks or other barriers operated by the Israeli military to control or restrict movement of Palestinians between villages and towns in the Occupied Territories. In many cases, Palestinians require permits issued by the Israeli authorities to be eligible to pass. Checkpoints cause immense travel delays and severely restrict movement. At the beginning of 2006, there were over 470 checkpoints and roadblocks in the West Bank alone.

Christian Zionism: The belief among some Christians that the return of the Jews to their ancestral lands, and the establishment of the state of Israel, is in accordance with biblical prophecy and a necessary prerequisite for Jesus' second coming. Advocating unquestioning support for the state of Israel, this belief holds that Jews have exclusive claims to the land of Palestine-Israel. Distinct from political Zionism, Christian Zionism is invested in a theological framework known as premillennial dispensationalism that does not necessarily hold sympathy for Jews as a people or Judaism as a religion but instead holds that some Jews will accept Christ as the Messiah in the final days while the rest perish.

Christianity: In Palestine-Israel Christianity can be grouped into four broad categories: 1) the Eastern Orthodox churches, such as Greek Orthodox communities who claim a continuous presence in the Holy Land since the times of the apostles; 2) the "Oriental" Orthodox churches, such as the Syrian, Coptic, and Armenian Orthodox communities; 3) the Catholic family of churches including Roman Catholic communities (referred to as the "Latin" church) as well as "Eastern Catholic" or "Eastern Rite Catholic" churches such as Greek Catholic (Melkite) or Syrian Catholic churches who, though in communion with Rome and recognizing the authority of the pope, have maintained their own distinctive liturgy and traditions, and outnumber the number of "Latin" Catholics in Palestine-Israel; 4) the various Protestant communities, including not only Anglican and Lutheran churches, present since the nineteenth century, but also independent evangelical churches, including Baptist, Pentecostal, and more. Today, of the roughly 3.8 million Palestinians living in the Occupied Territories, less than two percent are Christians. Of the 1.4 million Palestinians living inside Israel, roughly eight percent belong to Christian communities.

Church of the Holy Sepulcher: One of the most important sites in Christianity, where tradition holds the death, burial, and resurrection of Jesus Christ took place; located in the Old City of Jerusalem.

Closure: Israeli-imposed movement restrictions for Palestinian goods and labor. Closures are of unspecified duration, often imposed without explanation, and seriously disrupt daily life. They prevent Palestinians from reaching hospitals and other medical care, schools, and universities, as well as places of work and worship.

Convergence Plan (also called Realignment): The next phase in Israel's unilateral policy of "maximum territory, minimum Arabs" to ensure a demographic Jewish majority in Israel. Through this plan Israel proposes unilaterally to declare its borders over and against the Palestinians, relocating some 60,000 settlers from isolated settlements to major settlement blocs, annexing all areas west of the separation barrier including East Jerusalem and all major settlement blocs in the West Bank as well as the Jordan Valley, leaving isolated islands of land on forty to fifty percent of the West Bank for a future Palestinian state.

Curfew: A specific period of time (hours, days, weeks) imposed by the Israeli military on a community forcing its inhabitants to stay indoors, with occasional breaks to stock food and other supplies.

Diaspora: Often used in reference to Jewish communities outside the land of Israel; also used for other communities in exile from their homelands, including Palestinian communities outside of Palestine.

Disengagement Plan: Proposed by former Israeli Prime Minister Ariel Sharon, this unilateral initiative led to the evacuation of all Israeli settlers from and the dismantling of all settlements in the Gaza Strip (as well from four settlements in the northern West Bank), though maintaining effective control over Gaza (i.e., control over Gaza's borders, air, and sea space) and creating a reality of poverty and unemployment in what some call "one big prison" for the Palestinian residents of Gaza.

East Jerusalem: The area of pre-1967 Palestinian East Jerusalem municipal boundaries plus additional West Bank land belonging to some 28 surrounding villages occupied and subsequently annexed by Israel following the 1967 War.

Fatah: Acronym for Harakat At-Tahrir Al-Filistiniya (Palestinian Liberation Movement), with the first letters in reverse order. Formally founded in Kuwait in 1959 by Yasser Arafat and associates and headed by Arafat until his death in 2004. The largest and strongest PLO faction; advocates a democratic, secular, multi-religious state.

Final Status Negotiations: Provided for in the 1993 Declaration of Principles to be the second part of a two-phase timetable (first part to involve a five-year "interim" or "transitional" period during which Israel would withdraw from Palestinian centers in the Occupied Territories and transfer power to the Palestinians), and to cover issues including the following: Jerusalem, refugees, settlements, security arrangements, borders, and water resources. On May 4, 1999, the interim phase ended with no permanent status agreement in sight.

Fourth Geneva Convention: International agreement adopted in 1949 that delineates standards for the treatment of civilians under occupation, including their protection from degrading or dehumanizing treatment, coercion, torture, confiscation of property, and collective punishment. The Conventionforbids the transfer of part of the occupier's population to the occupied territory and ensures freedom of movement. Israel is a signatory to the Fourth Geneva Convention but refuses to recognize its applicability in the Occupied Territories.

Gaza Strip: Part of the Occupied Territories, with the Mediterranean Sea to the west, Egypt to the south, and Israel to the north and east. As home to nearly 1.4 million Palestinians, over two-thirds of whom are refugees, in a land area of only 140 square miles (ca. 363 square km), Gaza is one of the most densely populated areas in the world. Part of historical Palestine occupied by Egypt following the 1948 War and by Israel following the 1967 War.

Greater Jerusalem: Term used to refer to the inner metropolitan core around Jerusalem and beyond the Green Line where 300,000 Palestinians and 200,000 Israelis reside; includes twenty settlements beyond the city's municipal boundaries.

Green Line: Term used following Israel's occupation of the West Bank and Gaza in 1967 to refer to the post-1948 War ceasefire line (proper name is "1949 Armistice Line"), i.e., the "border" separating pre-1967 Israel from the Occupied Territories. The demarcation line (laid down in the Armistice Agreements of 1949) is the internationally recognized border.

Hamas: Acronym for Harakat Al-Muqawama Al-Islamiyya, the Palestinian Islamic Resistance Movement. Fundamentalist political movement grown out of religious associations—advocating for an Islamic state in all of historic Palestine—emerging shortly after the outbreak of the intifada in 1988. Hamas was initially tolerated, if not encouraged, by Israel as an alternative to the PLO. Gained popularity through charitable efforts and the provision of educational and health services. Has carried out many attacks on Israelis, including suicide bombings in Israeli cities killing and maiming civilians. Second to Fatah as largest Palestinian faction, yet gained a majority of seats in the 2006 Palestinian Legislative Council elections.

Al-Haram al-Sharif / Temple Mount: The Noble Sanctuary, one of the three most important sites in Islam, comprising nearly one-sixth of Jerusalem's Old City. Both Al-Aqsa Mosque and the Dome of the Rock are located on the compound, which in its entirety is regarded as a mosque. Jews refer to the area as Temple Mount, revering it as the location of the Second Temple, destroyed by the Romans.

Intifada: "Civil uprising" or, in Arabic, "shaking off." After decades of occupation, economic exploitation, and human rights violations, the Palestinian people began a collective uprising against the Israeli occupation in the Occupied Territories with the *first intifada* erupting in Gaza in December 1987. Demonstrations, rock throwing, strikes, boycotts of Israeli goods, tax resistance, and general unrest lasted for six years with the goal to end the Israeli occupation and establish Palestinian independence. The Israeli military responded with harsh measures: travel restrictions, military closures, limitations on the money that could be brought into the Occupied Territories, school and university closures, and mass arrests. With the signing of the Oslo accords, the intifada came to an end. The *second* or *al-Aqsa intifada* began in September 2000 when Likud opposition leader Ariel Sharon made a provocative visit to the Al-Aqsa Mosque, with thousands of security forces deployed in and around the Old City. The incident soon sparked a widespread uprising among Palestinians who had seen few benefits from the years of the Oslo process. After five years, the death toll among Palestinians had reached almost 4,000 with almost 30,000 injured and among Israelis over 1,000 dead with over 7,000 injured, causing unprecedented destruction to the Palestinian infrastructure and economy.

Islam: Monotheistic religion founded on the belief that God revealed the Holy Qur'an to the prophet Muhammad in Saudi Arabia in the seventh century CE. Among other things, Muslims can practice their faith by following the "Five Pillars" of Islam: Salah (prayer five times a day), Zakat (almsgiving to the poor), Shehadah (bearing witness that "there is no god but God and that Muhammad is the prophet of God"), the Hajj (making a pilgrimage to the holy cities of Mecca and Medina in Saudi Arabia), and Ramadan (ninth month of the Islamic calendar in which Muslims fast during the day).

Jewish National Fund (JNF): A multi-national organization founded in 1901 to purchase and develop land in Palestine for the use of Jews. After the 1948 War, Israel sold land to the JNF that had been confiscated from Palestinians with the purpose of preventing land from being sold to non-Jews.

Judaism: The oldest monotheistic religion in the world today, based on the Torah, the Jewish name for the first five books of the Hebrew Bible or Old Testament, as well as the books of the "prophets" and the "writings" also found in the Hebrew Bible, and including practices such as observing Shabbat (Sabbath) and keeping kosher. According to Jewish law, anyone born to a Jewish mother is automatically a Jew. Many Jews in Israel are secular and do not observe Jewish law. Israel also contains a wide variety of Jewish religious expression from Reform and Conservative to Modern Orthodox and ultra-Orthodox (often called haredi).

Kadima: Israeli political party formed in 2005 when former Prime Minister Ariel Sharon broke away from Likud to carry out his policy of unilateral disengagement; formally came to power in the Knesset in 2006. Now headed by Ehud Olmert.

Knesset: The Israeli parliament.

Labor: One of the major Israeli political parties. Originally called Mapai, the main Zionist socialist party in 1930; dominated Israeli political life during the 1950s and 1960s.

Law of Return: Israeli law that allows any Jew in the world to immigrate to Israel, declaring that Israel is a state of all of the Jewish people wherever they may be.

Likud: Parliamentary bloc representing the right-wing parties in Israel formed in 1973; apart from 1992-96, dominated Israeli political life from the late 1970s to 2005.

Mizrahi: Collective name for Jews coming from Arab countries to Palestine-Israel and who struggled against deprivation and discrimination. Since the 1970s the Mizrahim make up over half the Jewish population.

Nakba: Arabic for "catastrophe," referring to the events leading up to and following the 1948 War that led to the dispossession and expulsion of between 750,000 and 900,000 Palestinians.

Occupied Territories: Designates East Jerusalem, the West Bank, and the Gaza Strip, all territories militarily occupied by Israel since 1967. The Occupied Territories make up twenty-two percent of historical Palestine.

One-State Solution: Sees all of the territory of Palestine-Israel united as a single state as the solution to the conflict. This binational state would be a home for two peoples—Israelis and Palestinians—and instead of being a Jewish state (as Israel is now) or a Muslim state (as some Palestinians might desire), it would be a secular state with equal rights for all of its citizens.

Oslo Accords: Peace process that began with secret negotiations in Norway between PLO members and Israeli officials and led to the *Declaration of Principles (DoP)* in September 1993, outlining guidelines for future negotiations as well as for a Palestinian five-year interim autonomy in the Occupied Territories, followed by a permanent settlement based on UNSC Resolutions 242 and 338. Postponed difficult issues such as Jerusalem, refugees, settlements, water, security, and borders. The *Oslo I Agreement* signed in May 1994 outlined the first stage of Palestinian autonomy—in Gaza and Jericho—including Israeli redeployment and the establishment of a Palestinian self-government authority. Israel remained in control of the settlements, military locations, and security matters. The *Oslo II* or *Taba Agreement,* signed in September 1995. outlined the second stage of Palestinian autonomy, extending it to other parts of the West Bank, which is divided into three areas, A, B, and C. October 1997 was the target date for the completion of further redeployment and October 1999 for reaching a final status agreement. The stipulated interim period ended in May 1999 and triggered a heated debate among the Palestinians as to whether to declare unilaterally a Palestinian state.

Palestine-Israel: In this volume, Palestine-Israel refers to the land between the Jordan River to the east and the Mediterranean Sea to the west, today consisting of the state of Israel and the Occupied Territories.

Palestinian Authority (PA): Established on the basis of the Declaration of Principles signed by the PLO and Israel in 1993 and governs Palestinian affairs in the self-ruled areas of the Occupied Territories. It consists of an elected president, an appointed cabinet, and the Palestinian Legislative Council. The PA is subject to the agreements signed with Israel and as such has no foreign relation powers, and as a political body in the Occupied Territories, the PA does not represent Palestinian refugees in the diaspora.

Palestine Liberation Organization (PLO): Founded in May 1964 in Jerusalem. When Fatah, led by Yasser Arafat, took over the PLO in 1969, it became an umbrella organization for various Palestinian factions and acquired a more central role in mobilizing Palestinians as well as international support. The PLO created a number of organizations to provide education, health, and other relief services. In 1974, the PLO was recognized by the Arab League and the United Nations as the representative of the Palestinian people and was granted observer status by the UN. On November 15, 1988, it declared Palestinian independence, and in December 1988, it announced the recognition of Israel's right to exist and renounced terrorism. The PLO remains the representative of all Palestinians, in the Occupied Territories as well as the diaspora.

Palestinians: Arabs who live in or whose origins are in Palestine-Israel. Today it is estimated that there are close to 10 million Palestinians worldwide; roughly 3.8 million live in the Occupied Territories, 1.4 million live inside Israel, and the rest live in the diaspora with millions in refugee camps in Jordan, Lebanon, and Syria. At the beginning of the twentieth century, well over ninety percent of the people in historical Palestine were Palestinian Arab Christians and Muslims; today the population in Palestine-Israel is fast approaching a fifty percent Palestinian / fifty percent Israeli Jewish demographic balance.

Partition Plan (UNGA Resolution 181): On November 29, 1947, the United Nations General Assembly passed Resolution 181, the Partition Plan dividing Palestine into a Jewish and Arab state, with Jerusalem and Bethlehem as an international protectorate or *corpus separatum.* The plan granted the Jews fifty-six percent of Mandatory Palestine—at a time when they owned only six percent of the land—with a population of 498,000 Jews and 325,000 Palestinians, and the Palestinians forty-three percent of Palestine, with 807,000 Palestinian inhabitants and 10,000 Jewish inhabitants.

Refugees: It is estimated that there are more than seven million Palestinian refugees and internally displaced persons (IDPs: displaced Palestinians who remained in what became the state of Israel) today. The majority of Palestinian refugees and IDPs were displaced during the 1948 War when between 750,000 and 900,000 Palestinians were expelled from their homes. About 400,000 Palestinians were displaced, half for a second time, during the 1967 War. More than 500 Palestinian villages were depopulated and later destroyed to prevent the return of the refugees. Today more than one and a quarter million Palestinian refugees reside in fifty-nine official refugee camps located in the West Bank, Gaza Strip, Jordan, Lebanon, and Syria. The refugee camp remains a symbol of the temporary nature of exile and the demand to exercise the right of return.

Right of Return (UNGA Resolution 194): The United Nations General Assembly adopted Resolution 194 on December 11, 1948, stating the right of return: The refugees wishing to return to their homes and live at peace with their neighbors should be permitted to do so at the earliest practicable date, and that compensation should be paid for the property of those choosing not to return and for loss of or damage to property which, under principles of international law or in equity, should be made good by the Governments or authorities responsible.

Road Map: Plan put together by the Quartet—the United States, the United Nations, the European Union, and Russia—in December 2002 aimed at a "final comprehensive settlement of the Israeli-Palestinian conflict by 2005," based on a two-state solution, starting with an end to terrorism and a freeze on Israeli settlements and other steps to normalize conditions. Though still espoused by the Quartet, the Road Map is largely considered to be irrelevant due to Israeli unilateralism.

Separation Barrier: Also referred to as "Wall" or "Fence," Israel began construction of this barrier, composed of fences, trenches, and concrete walls built mostly inside the West Bank, in 2002 on the pretext of security. Its construction, which drew international opposition, cuts deep into Palestinian territory and involves the confiscation of large amounts of fertile Palestinian land, the "ghettoization" of Palestinian towns and villages, and cutting off thousands of Palestinians from social services, schools, and their farmlands. Many predictions see the barrier stretching up to 680 km (430 miles), directly affecting over twenty percent of the West Bank population (who will either be separated from their lands or isolated between the barrier and the Green Line), and leaving ten percent of the West Bank under exclusive Israeli control. In June 2004 the *International Court of Justice* ruled that construction of the barrier was illegal under international law because it involves destruction and/or confiscation of Palestinian property and imposes severe restrictions on Palestinian movement and that Israel should cease construction, return seized property, and compensate affected Palestinian landowners.

Sephardi (Hebrew for a person living in Spain): Collective name given to Jews from Middle Eastern/Arab countries.

Settlements: In violation of the Fourth Geneva Conventions, Israeli citizens relocated to the Occupied Territories following the 1967 War in a process of colonization deemed illegal by the international community. The intention is to create "facts on the ground" that fulfill Israel's goals of gaining more territory. Today over 450,000 Israeli settlers live in illegal settlements and outposts in the West Bank, including 200,000 in occupied East Jerusalem. The majority live in large settlement blocs such as Gush Etzion in the southern West Bank, Ma'ale Adumim and Givat Ze'ev around Jerusalem, and Ariel in the northern West Bank.

Shoah: Hebrew for "calamity" and name given to the Holocaust in Europe in which the Nazi regime systematically murdered about six million Jews.

Torah: Hebrew word for the Law revealed to Moses on Mt. Sinai; often refers to the first five books of the Old Testament.

Transfer: A form of ethnic cleansing in which a population is displaced from a particular territory because of religion, ethnicity, nationality, or another identifying feature that sets it apart as "undesirable" by the dominant power; a term used to describe the ethnic cleansing that occurred during the 1948 and 1967 wars in which Palestinians were expelled from their homes.

Two-State Solution: Sees the creation of two separate independent states—the state of Israel and the state of Palestine—as the solution to the conflict. Under this solution, Israel would end its occupation of and withdraw from the Occupied Territories, with Palestinians forming a state on these territories. For Palestinians this solution can only be economically viable and meet the minimum demands of justice if the Palestinian State comprises all of the West Bank, including East Jerusalem, and the Gaza Strip (twenty-two percent of historical Palestine). Ongoing Israeli colonization of the Occupied Territories is making the implementation of this solution increasingly difficult.

United Nations Relief and Works Agency for Palestine Refugees in the Near East (UNRWA): Established in 1949 to give emergency assistance to Palestinians displaced by the 1948 War and began to operate in May 1950. Its mandate is to provide essential education, health, and relief services to Palestine refugees living in Jordan, Lebanon, Syria, and the Occupied Territories.

Wailing Wall: One of the most important sites in Judaism, located in the Old City of Jerusalem, believed to be the western wall of the Second Temple.

War of 1967: Also June or Six-Day War; launched by an Israeli attack on Egyptian posts on June 5, 1967. Also referred to as *An-Naksa*, the setback. Resulted in the Israeli occupation of the rest of Palestine, i.e., the Gaza Strip and West Bank, including East Jerusalem. Israel illegally declared its jurisdiction over all the Occupied Territories on June 27 and formally annexed East Jerusalem on June 28, 1967. *United Nations Security Council Resolution 242*, adopted on November 22, 1967, called on Israel to withdraw its army from territories occupied in the course of the War of 1967. *United Nations Security Council Resolution 338*, adopted on October 22, 1973, called for the immediate implementation of UNSC Resolution 242 with a view to establishing peace.

War of 1948: After Britain ended its mandate, Israel declared independence on May 14, 1948, after which war broke out between Israeli forces and Arab armies. By the end of the war, Israel gained control of seventy-eight percent of British Mandatory Palestine, including fifty-four percent of areas designated for the Palestinian Arab state. Palestine is fragmented as Jordan and Egypt held the West Bank and the Gaza Strip respectively,

Jerusalem was divided, and Palestinian society was dismantled and its people rendered a nation of displaced refugees with 750,000-900,000 Palestinians displaced before, during, and after the fighting, not allowed to return, with 150,000 Palestinians remaining in new state of Israel. Over 500 Palestinian villages were depopulated and destroyed.

West Bank: The west bank of the Jordan River, part of the Occupied Territories, with Jenin in the north and Hebron in the south, with Jerusalem and Bethlehem centrally located and the Jordan River in the east. Part of historical Palestine occupied by Jordan following the 1948 War and by Israel following the 1967 War.

West Bank Areas A, B, and C: These are jurisdictional divisions created in the West Bank in 1995, with the Oslo II Agreement. Area A (seventeen percent), comprising Palestinian urban centers, came under PA administrative and internal security responsibility. Area B (twenty-four percent) remained under Israeli military control with PA control over civilian affairs. Area C (fifty-nine percent) remained under Israeli military and civilian control.

Zionism: Nationalist movement that emerged in Europe in the late nineteenth-century seeking to solve the problem of anti-Judaism that European Jewish communities had faced for centuries. Early Zionist leaders like the Austrian Theodor Herzl advocated for the creation of a Jewish state for the Jewish nation.

Adapted from glossaries from PASSIA Diary 2006 (Jerusalem: Palestinian Academic Society for the Study of International Affairs, 2006) and from Ilan Pappé, *A History of Modern Palestine: One Land, Two Peoples* (Cambridge: Cambridge University Press, 2004).

Resources for Further Study

MCC RESOURCES

MCC DVD/Videos

MCC DVD/videos are available for purchase or for free borrowing from any MCC office or via the MCC website, www.mcc.org.

Walking the Path Jesus Walked. MCC, 2002. Hear Christians from Syria, Palestine, and Egypt share their faith, and learn about the enduring, vibrant witness of the historic Christian churches in the Middle East.

The Dividing Wall. MCC, 2004. Features Palestinians whose lives have been devastated by Israel's separation barrier and highlights the voices of Palestinians and Israelis who work for a future of bridges instead of walls.

Children of the Nakba. MCC, 2005. For Palestinians, the events between 1947 and 1949 are remembered as a time when Israeli military forces destroyed over 500 Palestinian villages and expelled between 700,000 and 900,000 Palestinians from their lands. These refugees have lived exiled from their land since then. Today Palestinians represent one-third of the global refugee and internally displaced population. Learn about the Palestinians who call these events the *Nakba*, an Arabic word meaning catastrophe.

MCC PUBLICATIONS

*Available as hard copies through any MCC office or through the
MCC catalogue at www.mcc.org/catalog. Many are
also available online.*

"Peacebuilding in Palestine / Israel: A Discussion Paper" meant to
help facilitate a conversation in communities back in North
America about stewardship, divestment, and economic justice, online at www.mcc.org/papers/2005-05_Peacebuild-
ing_in_Palestine-Israel.pdf

"Christian Zionism and Peace in the Holy Land." *MCC Peace Office
Newsletter* 35/3. July-September 2005. www.mcc.org/re-
spub/pon/PON_2005-07-01.pdf

"Walling Off the Future for Palestinians and Israelis." *MCC Peace
Office Newsletter* 34/3. July-September 2004. www.mcc.org/
respub/pon/mcc_pon04_03.pdf

"Country Profile: Occupied Palestinian Territories." *A Common
Place*. September/October 2004 (including the *Hello* publication for children): www.mcc.org/acp/2004/sept_oct/
acp_septoct2004.pdf

Epp Weaver, Alain. "Constantinianism, Zionism, Diaspora: Toward
a Theology of Exile and Return." MCC Occasional Paper #28,
2002. www.mcc.org/respub/occasional/28.html.

———— and Sonia Weaver, *Salt and Sign: Mennonite Central Committee
in Palestine, 1949-1999* (Akron, Pa.: MCC, 1999).

Weaver, Sonia K. *What Is Palestine-Israel? Answers to Common Questions.* Scottdale, Pa.: Herald Press, 2007

For regularly updated information about MCC's work in Palestine-
Israel, visit www.mcc.org/palestine/

OTHER RESOURCES

HISTORY AND CONTEXT

Aruri, Naseer, ed. *Palestinian Refugees: The Right of Return*. London:
Pluto Press, 2001.

————. *Dishonest Broker: America's Role in Israel and Palestine*. Cambridge: South End Press, 2003.

Atallah, Susan and Toine van Teeffelen, eds. *The Wall Cannot Stop
Our Stories: Diaries from Palestine 2000-2004*. Bethlehem: Terra
Sancta School for Girls, Sisters of St. Joseph, 2004.

Benvenisti, Meron. *Sacred Landscape: Buried History of the Holy Land Since 1948.* Berkeley: University of California Press, 2001.

Carey, Roane, ed. *The New Intifada: Resisting Israel's Apartheid.* London: Verso Books, 2001.

———and Jonathan Shainin, eds. *The Other Israelis: Voices of Refusal and Dissent.* New York: New Press, 2002.

Halper, Jeff. *Obstacles to Peace: A Re-Framing of the Palestinian-Israeli Conflict.* 3rd. ed. Jerusalem: Israeli Committee Against House Demolitions, 2005.

Hass, Amira. *Drinking the Sea at Gaza: Days and Nights in a Land under Siege.* New York: Henry Holt & Co, 1998.

———. *Reporting from Ramallah: An Israeli Journalist in an Occupied Land.* Cambridge: MIT Press, 2003.

Khalidi, Rashid. *Palestinian Identity: The Construction of Modern National Consciousness.* New York: Columbia University Press, 1997.

———. *The Iron Cage: The Story of the Palestinian Struggle for Statehood.* Boston: Beacon Press, 2006.

Khalidi, Walid. *All That Remains: The Palestinian Villages Occupied and Depopulated by Israel in 1948.* Washington, D.C.: Institute for Palestine Studies, 1992.

Morris, Benny. *The Birth of the Palestinian Refugee Problem, 1947-1949 Revisited.* Cambridge: Cambridge University Press, 2003.

———. *1948 and After: Israel and the Palestinians.* Oxford: Clarendon Press, 1994.

Masalha, Nur. *Expulsion of the Palestinians: The Concept of 'Transfer' in Zionist Political Thought, 1882-1948.* Washington, D.C.: Institute for Palestine Studies, 1992.

———. *A Land Without a People: Israel, Transfer, and the Palestinians 1949-1985.* London: Faber and Faber, 1997.

———. *Politics of Denial: Israel and the Palestinian Refugee Problem.* London: Pluto Press, 2003.

Neff, Donald. *Fallen Pillars: U.S. Policy Toward Palestine and Israel since 1945.* Washington, D.C.: Institute for Palestine Studies, 1995.

Pappé, Ilan. *A History of Modern Palestine: One Land, Two Peoples.* Cambridge: Cambridge University Press, 2004.

———. *The Ethnic Cleansing of Palestine.* Oxford: Oneworld Publications, 2006.

Reinhart, Tanya. *Israel/Palestine: How to End the War of 1948.* New York: Seven Stories Press, 2002.

———. *The Road Map to Nowhere: Israel/Palestine Since 2003.* London: Verso, 2006.

Roy, Sara. *Failing Peace: Gaza and the Palestinian-Israeli Conflict.* London: Pluto Press, 2006.

Said, Edward W. *The Question of Palestine.* New York: Vintage, 1992.

———. *End of the Peace Process.* New York: Pantheon, 2000.

———. *From Oslo to Iraq and the Road Map.* New York: Pantheon, 2004.

Shlaim, Avi. *The Iron Wall: Israel and the Arab World.* New York: W. W. Norton & Company, 1999.

BIBLICAL / THEOLOGICAL STUDIES:

Ateek, Naim Stifan. *Justice and Only Justice: A Palestinian Theology of Liberation.* Maryknoll, N.Y.: Orbis Books, 1989.

Brueggemann, Walter. *The Land: Place as Gift, Promise and Challenge in Biblical Faith.* 2nd. ed. Minneapolis: Fortress, 2002.

———. *The Prophetic Imagination.* 2nd. ed. Minneapolis: Fortress Press, 2001.

Burge, Gary M. *Whose Land? Whose Promise? What Christians Are Not Being Told About Israel and the Palestinians.* Cleveland: Pilgrim Press, 2003.

Chacour, Elias. *Blood Brothers.* Grand Rapids: Chosen Books, 2003.

———. *We Belong to the Land: The Story of a Palestinian Israeli who Lives for Peace and Reconciliation.* New York: HarperCollins, 1990.

Chapman, Colin. *Whose Promised Land?* Grand Rapids: Baker House, 2002.

Cragg, Kenneth. *The Arab Christian: A History in the Middle East.* Louisville: Westminster John Knox Press, 1991.

Crosby, Michael H. *Thy Will Be Done: Praying the Our Father as Subversive Activity.* Maryknoll, N.Y.: Orbis Books, 1977.

Ellis, Marc. *Toward a Jewish Theology of Liberation.* Maryknoll, N.Y.: Orbis Books, 1987.

———. *Out of the Ashes.* London: Pluto Press, 2002.

Friesen, LeRoy. *Mennonite Witness in the Middle East: A Missiological Introduction.* Elkhart, Ind.: Mennonite Board of Missions, 2000.

Frykholm, Amy Johnson. *Rapture Culture:* Left Behind *in Evangelical America.* Oxford: Oxford University Press, 2004.

Gorenberg, Gershom. *The End of Days: Fundamentalism and the Struggle for the Temple Mount.* Oxford: Oxford University Press, 2002.

Habel, Norman C. *The Land Is Mine: Six Biblical Land Ideologies.* Minneapolis: Fortress Press, 1995.

Halsell, Grace. *Forcing God's Hand: Why Millions Pray for a Quick Rapture . . . and the Destruction of the Planet.* Beltsville, Md.: Amana Publications, 1999.

Hill, Craig C. *In God's Time: The Bible and The Future.* Grand Rapids: Wm. B. Eerdmans Publishing Company, 2002.

Hubers, John. *Christian Zionism: A Historical Analysis and Critique.* Reformed Church of America, 2004. Available online at www.rca.org/synod/christianzionism.html.

Jeschke, Marlin. *Rethinking Holy Land: A Study in Salvation Geography.* Scottdale, Pa.: Herald Press, 2005.

Prior, Michael. *The Bible and Colonialism: A Moral Critique.* Sheffield, England: Sheffield Academic Press, 1997.

———, ed. *Speaking the Truth About Zionism and Israel.* London: Melisende, 2004.

Raheb, Mitri. *I Am a Palestinian Christian.* Minneapolis: Fortress Press, 1995.

———. *Bethlehem Besieged: Stories of Hope in Times of Trouble.* Minneapolis: Fortress Press, 2004.

Rantisi, Audeh G. and Ralph K. Beebe. *Blessed are the Peacemakers: A Palestinian Christian in the Occupied West Bank.* Grand Rapids: Zondervan, 1990.

Rossing, Barbara R. *The Rapture Exposed: The Message of Hope in the Book of Revelation.* Boulder, Col.: Westview Press, 2005.

Ruether, Rosemary Radford and Herman Ruether. *The Wrath of Jonah: The Crisis of Religious Nationalism in the Israeli-Palestinian Conflict.* New York: HarperCollins, 1989.

Sizer, Stephen. *Christian Zionism: Road Map to Armageddon?* Leicester, England: Inter-Varsity Press, 2004.

Wagner, Donald E. *Anxious for Armageddon: A Call to Partnership for Middle Eastern and Western Christians.* Scottdale, Pa.: Herald Press, 1995.

————. *Dying in the Land of Promise: Palestine and Palestinian Christianity from Pentecost to 2000.* London: Melisende, 2003.

Weber, Timothy P. *On the Road to Armageddon: How Evangelicals Became Israel's Best Friend.* Grand Rapids: Baker, 2004.

Yoder, John Howard. *The Jewish-Christian Schism Revisited,* ed. Michael G. Cartwright and Peter Ochs. Grand Rapids: Wm. B. Eerdmans, 2003.

————. *The Politics of Jesus.* 2nd. ed. Grand Rapids: Wm. B. Eerdmans, 1994.

INTERNET

Middle East News

Haaretz (Israel): www.haaretz.com

International Middle East Media Center (Palestine): www.imemc.org

Jerusalem Post (Israel): www.jpost.com

Maan Independent News Agency (Palestine): maannews.net/english

Palestine News Network (Palestine): www.palestinenet.org/english

Today in Palestine (Palestine): www.theheadlines.org

YnetNews—Yedioth Ahronoth (Israel): www.ynetnews.com/home/0,7340,L-3083,00.html

Middle East Commentary and Analysis

Americans for Middle East Understanding: www.ameu.org/index.asp

Challenging Christian Zionism: www.christianzionism.org

Christian Peacemaker Teams (CPT): www.cpt.org

Churches for Middle East Peace: www.cmep.org/index.html

Ecumenical Accompaniment Program in Israel and Palestine (EAPPI): www.eappi.org/eappiweb.nsf/index.htm

Evangelicals for Middle East Understanding: www.emeu.net

Foundation for Middle East Understanding: www.fmep.org

If Americans Knew: www.ifamericansknew.org

Middle East Research and Information Project (MERIP): www.merip.org

The Holy Land Christian Ecumenical Foundation: www.hcef. org/hcef/index.cfm/ID/2.cfm

U.S. Campaign to End the Occupation: www.endtheoccupation.org

UN Office for the Coordination of Humanitarian Affairs (OCHA): www.humanitarianinfo.org/opt

Washington Report on Middle East Affairs (WRMEA): www.washington-report.org

Palestinian Sites

Adalah—The Legal Center for Arab Minority Rights in Israel: www.adalah.org/eng/index.php

Al-Awda—The Palestinian Right of Return Coalition: www.al-awda.org

The Electronic Intifada (ei): electronicintifada.net/new.shtml

MIFTAH—Palestine Initiative for the Promotion of Global Dialogue and Democracy: www.miftah.org

Open Bethlehem: www.openbethlehem.org

Palestine Chronicle Weekly Journal: www.palestinechronicle.com

Palestine Monitor: www.palestinemonitor.org

Palestine Remembered: www.palestineremembered.com

PLO Negotiations Affairs Department: www.nad-plo.org/index. php

Jewish Sites

Americans for Peace Now: www.peacenow.org

B'tselem—The Israeli Information Center for Human Rights: www. btselem.org/English

Gush Shalom—Israeli Peace Bloc: zope.gush-shalom.org/home/en

Jewish Voice for Peace: www.jewishvoiceforpeace.org

Machsom Watch: www.machsomwatch.org

New Profile: www.newprofile.org

Not in My Name: www.nimn.org

Occupation Magazine: www.kibush.co.il/index.asp?lang=1

PEACE NOW: www.peacenow.org.il/site/en/homepage.asp?pi=25

Rabbis for Human Rights: www.rhr.israel.net

Refuse Solidarity Network: www.refusesolidarity.org

The Other Israel: otherisrael.home.igc.org

Tikkun—A Jewish Magazine, an Interfaith Movement: www.tikkun. org

Yesh Gvul: www.yeshgvul.org/english

Joint Palestinian-Israeli Sites

The Alternative Information Center: www..alternativenews.org

Bitterlemons.org—Palestinian-Israeli Crossfire: www.bitterlemons. org

Coalition of Women for Peace: www.coalitionofwomen.org/home/ english

Israel/Palestine Center for Research and Information: www.ipcri. org

Neve Shalom—Wahat al-Salaam www.nswas.com

The Parents' Circle—Families Forum: www.theparentscircle.com

Ta'ayush: www.taayush.org

Women in Black: www.womeninblack.org

MCC Palestine Partner Organizations

Anti-Apartheid Wall Campaign: www.stopthewall.org

Applied Research Institute—Jerusalem: www.arij.org

BADIL Resource Center for Palestinian Residency and Refugees' Rights: www.badil.org

Culture and Free Thought Association: www.palnet.com/~cfta

Holy Land Trust: www.holylandtrust.org

Israeli Committee Against House Demolitions: www.icahd.org/ eng

The Palestinian Center for Rapprochement between People: www.pcr.ps

PENGON—Palestinian Environmental NGOs Network: www.pen-gon.org

Sabeel Ecumenical Liberation Theology Center: www.sabeel.org

The East Jerusalem YMCA: www.ej-ymca.org/site

Wi'am Palestinian Conflict Resolution Center: www.planet.edu/ ~alaslah

Zochrot Association—Remembering the Nakba: www.nakbain-hebrew.org

Scripture Index

Genesis

1	40
1-11	52
2:24	72
3	51-52
8:21	52
11:1-9	52
12:1-3	52
12:7	49, 50
12:17	53
13:14-18	50
14:18-20	53
15:18-21	50
18:18-19	52
18:22-33	53
20:1-18	53
20:17-18	53
22:18	52
23:3-16	53
26:3-4	52, 50
28:13	50
35:12	50

Exodus

6:8	50
15	112
22:21-24	86, 87, 91-92
23:6	89

Leviticus

19:33-34	42, 46
25	40-41
25:2-5	95
25:8-17	81
25:18-23	95
26:31-34	54

Deuteronomy 66

1:8	50
4:1	41
4:6	41
6:10	50
7:1-2	62, 64
10:17-19	42, 46
24:1-4	71
24:17-22	42, 46
25:19	67
28:62-64	54

Joshua 14, 39, 53, 67-68, 69, 70-71, 72, 73

6:17	64
6:21	64
6:27	64
10:28	65
10:30	65
10:31	65
10:34	65
10:37	65
10:38	65
10:40	65
11:11	65
11:12	65
11:14	65
11:15	65
13-24	66
24:11-14	66

Judges 14, 39

1 Samuel 15:3 67

1 Kings

21	44, 80-84
21:3	81

21:7	81	29:10-14	132, 134
21:15	81	30:10-22	132
21:19	81	31:1-17	132
2 Kings	111, 115	**Ezekiel**	122
6	109-110, 116	28:25-26	132
6:21	109	34:11-31	132
6:22	109	36	132
		36:25-27	134
Psalms		37	132
24:1	38	37:11	133
37:11	58	37:24-25	134
119:172	157	38-39	120, 121
		40-48	132
Proverbs			
25:21	103	**Daniel**	122, 127
25:21-22	110	7:24	120
Isaiah	115	**Hosea**	
2:2-4	136	1:10-11	132, 137
5:1-7	139	2:21-23	137
5:8	43	11:10-11	132
11:11-16	132		
11:16	134	**Amos**	
25:6-8	136	6:1-7	54
32:2	111	9:11-15	132
32:15-16	111		
32:17-18	111	**Micah**	101, 115
35:8	134	2:1-3	43
35:8-10	132	2:2	75
40:1-11	137	4:1-4	99
40:3	136	4:3b-4	110, 111
40:27	133	4:4	13, 150
43:1-7	132		
49:22	130	**Zechariah**	
56:3-8	136	1:14-17	132
61:1-2	43	8:1-8	132
		10:8-12	132
Jeremiah	130		
7:1-15	54	**Matthew**	
23:3-8	132, 134	3:3	136
29:7	45	4:17	155

5:1-10	153
5:4	156
5:44	71
5:5	58, 100, 157
5:6	157
5:7	158
5:8	158
5:9	158
5:10	159
6:10	155
7:20	118
21:33-43	138
24	123
24:1-2	57
24:32-35	135
24:36	124
24:45-51	124
25	147
25:1-30	124
28:18-20	58

Mark

1:2-3	136
12:1-12	138
12:25	125
13	123
13:1-2	57
13:28-31	135
13:32	124
13:33-37	124

Luke

1:67-79	135
1:68-79	136
2:15	156
3:4-6	136
4:18-19	41, 43
17:21	155
20:9-19	138
21	123
21:5-6, 20-24	57
21:9-11	118

21:23-24, 28	135
21:29-33	135
23:43	126
24:39	124
24:41-43	124

John

1:23	136
1:5	160
3:16	89, 90
8:39-47	139
20:27	124

Acts 58

1:6	135
1:6-8	137
1:8	135
10:34-35	145
28:23-28	139

Romans

3:1-4	138
4:11-12	58
4:13	59
4:13-14	59
9:4-5	58
9:6-8	59
9:24	137
9:25-26	137
11	138
11:1	138
11:17	146
11:17-24	138
11:18	146
11:20	146
11:22	146
11:24	138
11:25-27	138
11:25-32	121
11:28-29	138
11:30	146
11:33-36	146-147

12	115	20:4-15	122
12:14-21	110	21:1-4	128
14:17	155	6-18	121

1 Corinthians
13:12	126
15:12-23	124
15:35-49	125

2 Corinthians
3:14-15	73

Galatians
3:6-9	59
3:8-9, 14	59
3:26-29	145
3:27-29	138

Ephesians 146
2:11-14	145
2:11-22	138
2:14	143
2:15	145

Colossians
3:9-11	47

1 Thessalonians
3:1-5	127
4:13	127
4:16-17	121, 127
4:18	127

Hebrews
8:13	139

Revelation 122, 127, 184
9:13-19	120
13:1	120
16:16	121
16:12	120

Subject Index

A

Abraham, 14, 39, 44, 49- 63,
139, 145
Al-Aqsa Martyrs Brigade, 107
Anti-Judaism, 14, 18, 23-24, 55-
56, 104, 108, 139-141, 146
Anti-Semitism. *See* Anti-Ju-
daism
Applied Research
Institute–Jerusalem, 11,
101, 102, 187
Ascherman, Arik, 92-93, 157
Ateek, Naim, 40, 44-48, 67, 70-
71, 74, 88-94, 183
Awad, Alex, 118-119, 123, 129,
144, 150

B

Balfour Declaration, 24, 26,
162, 168
Beatitudes, 153-160
Ben-Gurion, David, 27-28, 89,
93
*Borders and Bridges: Mennonite
Witness in a Religiously Di-
verse World*, 15
British Mandate, 18, 24-27,
162-163, 168, 175-176
B'Tselem, 115, 186

C

Camp David accords, 25, 165
Canaan, conquest. *See* Joshua
and the conquest of
Canaan
Chacour, Elias, 40, 79-80, 85,
151, 154-155, 160-161, 183

Christian Peacemaker Teams,
68, 185
Christian Zionism, 13-14, 39,
50-51, 61, 97, 108, 117-124,
129-132, 143-145, 150, 152,
169, 181, 184-185
Christians in Palestine-Israel,
14, 67- 71, 80, 97-101, 113,
143-152, 169, 183, 184, 185
Churches for Middle East
Peace, 47, 167, 185
Colonialism, 15-18, 22-23, 26,
73, 74, 184
Crusades, 15, 66

D

Darby, John Nelson, 119
Deir Yassin, 27, 63
Duaybis, Cedar, 150
Dula, Peter, 15

E

East Jerusalem, 25, 29, 31, 78,
98, 101, 105, 157, 164-166,
170, 177-178
East Jerusalem YMCA, 101,
157, 187
End times theology, 14, 17, 97,
117-142, 184-185

F

Families Forum, 112, 156-157,
187
Fatah, 33, 164, 167, 170, 175
Fence/wall, security. *See* Separation barrier (walls,
fences)

G

Gaza-Israeli disengagement, 32, 34, 167, 170, 173
Gush Emunim, 68-69
Gutiérrez, Gustavo, 46

H

Hagee, John, 117, 129, 130, 141
Hamas, 32-33, 107, 167, 171-172
Herzl, Theodor, 23, 55, 162, 179
Hezbollah, 33
Holocaust, 15, 24, 55-56, 60, 104, 140, 163, 177
House demolitions, 29, 77, 82-83, 92, 157, 158

I

International Christian Embassy of Jerusalem, 50, 61, 130-131, 135, 141
Intifada, 29- 31, 103-104, 165-166, 172, 182, 186
Islamic Jihad, 107
Israel – founding, 21-37, 62, 104, 163
Israeli Committee Against House Demolitions (ICAHD), 85, 158, 187
Israeli settlements. *See* Settlements, Israeli

J

Jeschke, Marlin, 39-40, 47, 184
Jesus Christ, 10, 16, 41-44, 47, 51, 57-60, 70- 73, 89-90, 93, 100, 115, 118, 121-127, 131, 134-139, 144-161, 169, 180, 185
Joshua and the conquest of Canaan, 14, 16, 39, 45, 50, 53, 62-74

K

Khalidi, Rashid, 27, 37, 182
Kimmerling, Baruch, 56, 61

L

Land, theology of, 14-17, 38-74, 80-90, 93-96, 99-101, 109-112, 144-147, 181- 184
Late Great Planet Earth, The. See Lindsey, Hal
Law of Return, Israeli, 28, 47, 164, 173
League of Nations, 24, 26, 162
Lebanon/Gaza war (2006), 33, 167
Lebanon, Israeli invasion of (1982), 165
Left Behind novel series, 14, 184
Lindsey, Hal, 119-120, 135, 141

M

Mecca agreement, 167
Mennonite Central Committee (MCC), 11, 15-16, 36, 47, 93, 101, 115, 151-152, 180, 181, 187, 199, 200
Mennonites, 14-18, 116, 160, 183, 199, 200
Militarization, Israeli, 106-108, 113, 115
Morris, Benny, 55, 61, 73, 182

N

Nakba, 15, 21-23, 26-37, 47, 62-63, 72-76, 159, 174, 180, 187
Names and name debates, 17-18, 22, 28, 73, 159
New Profile, 112-116, 186

O

October War. *See* Yom Kippur War

Oslo Accords, 30-32, 165-166, 172, 174, 179, 183
Ottoman Empire, 18, 23-26, 83, 162, 168

P

Palestine Liberation Organization (PLO), 29-33, 107, 164-166, 170-175, 186
Palestine—refugees. *See* Refugees, Palestinian
Palestinian Authority, 30-33, 166-167, 175
Palestinian Christians. *See* Christians in Palestine-Israel
Palestinian resistance to occupation, 29-31, 107-108. *See also* Intifada
Pappé, Ilan, 28, 30, 34-37, 167, 179, 182
Paul, Apostle, 58-59, 73, 110, 115, 124-126, 137-140, 145-147, 155
Peaceful alternatives, 35-36, 47, 90-93, 109-116, 153-161

R

Rabbis for Human Rights, 92, 157, 186
Raheb, Mitri, 40, 100-102, 113, 116, 184
Ramadan War. *See* Yom Kippur War
Rantisi, Audeh, 62-63, 73, 85, 90-94, 184
Refugees, Palestinian, 15-16, 22, 27-30, 34-36, 47, 60-63, 76-85, 91, 105, 159, 163-164, 171, 174-182, 187

S

Sabeel Ecumenical Liberation Theological Center, 150, 151, 187
Sabra and Shatila refugee camp massacre, 165
Said, Edward, 15, 35, 183
Security fence/wall. *See* Separation barrier (walls, fences)
Separation barrier (walls, fences), 32, 34, 38-39, 51, 69, 77-78, 83, 88, 90-93, 96-98, 105-107, 114, 145, 149, 151, 156-158, 161, 166-167, 170, 176-177, 180-181, 187
Settlements, Israeli, 28-34, 51-52, 68-69, 77-78, 83, 88, 91-92, 97-98, 117-118, 164-167, 170-177
Sharon, Ariel, 31-32, 166-167, 170-173
Shlaim, Avi, 28, 35, 37, 183
Six-Day War of 1967, 25, 29, 76-77, 91, 98-99, 164, 170-171, 176-179
Suez War, 164

T

Tamarin, Georges R., 67-68, 74
Terrorism, 25-26, 107, 165, 172, 175-176

U

Unemployment, Palestinian, 33, 39, 49, 78, 87, 96-97, 105, 149, 156, 170
United Nations and Palestine-Israel, 24-29, 47, 77, 91, 163-165, 175-178

W

Wall Cannot Stop Our Stories, The, 158, 161, 181

Wall/fence, security. *See* Separation barrier (walls, fences)

War of 1948, 18, 21-28, 35, 62-63, 72-76, 91, 159, 178-179, 182, 183

War of 1967. *See* Six-Day War of 1967

War of 1973. *See* Yom Kippur War

Water resource issues, 10, 16, 30-31, 49, 83, 96, 98, 101-102, 171, 174

Wi'am Palestinian Conflict Resolution Center, 159, 187

Y

YMCA, East Jerusalem. *See* East Jerusalem YMCA

Yoder, John Howard, 45-48, 185

Yom Kippur War, 164

Z

Zionism, 14-15, 21-26, 34-35, 55-56, 63-64, 72, 89, 92-93, 162-163, 179, 181, 184

Zochrot, 26, 36, 72-74, 102, 159, 187

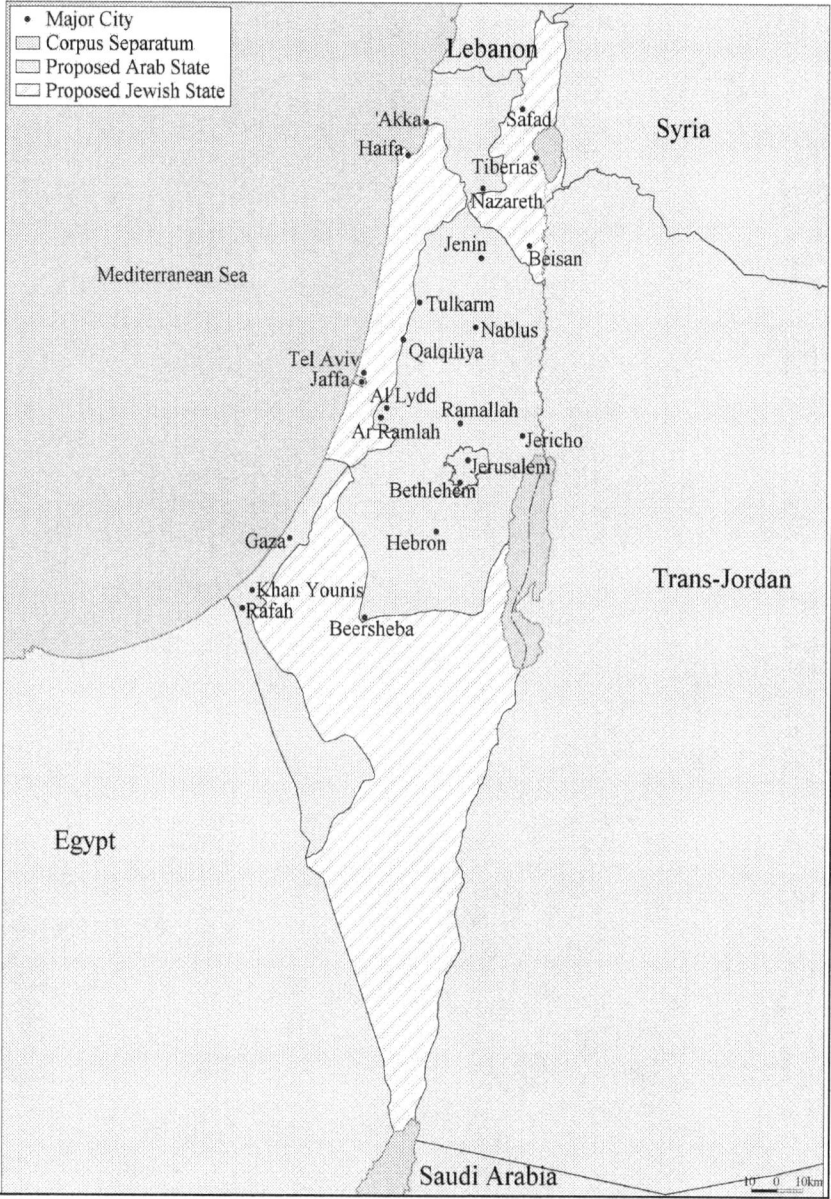

United Nations Partition Plan, 1947

- Major City
- Corpus Separatum
- Proposed Arab State
- Proposed Jewish State

Lebanon

Syria

'Akka
Haifa
Safad
Tiberias
Nazareth

Jenin
Beisan

Mediterranean Sea

Tulkarm
Nablus
Qalqiliya
Tel Aviv
Jaffa
Al Lydd
Ramallah
Ar Ramlah
Jericho
Jerusalem
Bethlehem

Gaza
Hebron

Trans-Jordan

Khan Younis
Rafah
Beersheba

Egypt

Saudi Arabia

10   0   10km

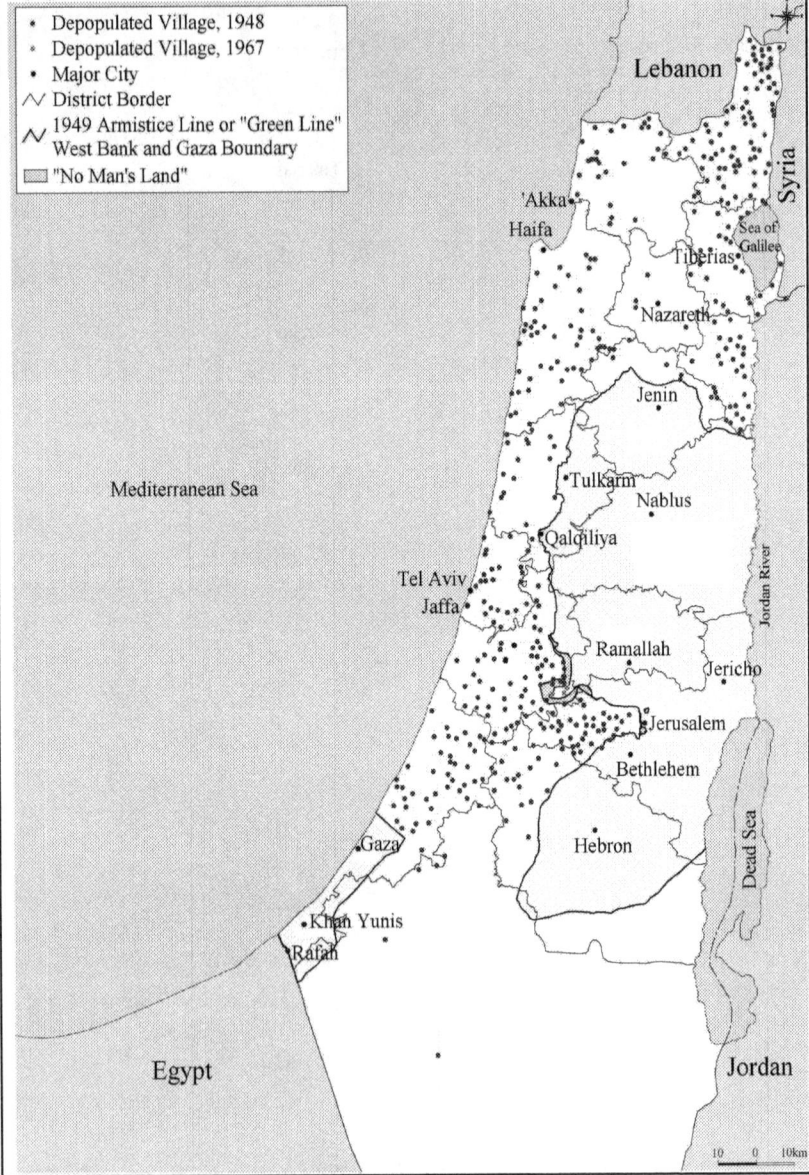

Depopulated Palestinian Villages in 1948 and 1967

- Depopulated Village, 1948
- Depopulated Village, 1967
- Major City
- District Border
- 1949 Armistice Line or "Green Line"
  West Bank and Gaza Boundary
- "No Man's Land"

Lebanon

Syria

'Akka

Haifa

Sea of
Galilee

Tiberias

Nazareth

Jenin

Mediterranean Sea

Tulkarm

Nablus

Qalqiliya

Jordan River

Tel Aviv

Jaffa

Ramallah

Jericho

Jerusalem

Bethlehem

Dead Sea

Gaza

Hebron

Khan Yunis

Rafah

Egypt

Jordan

10   0   10km

Israel and the Occupied Palestinian Territories

- Major City
- 1949 Armistice Line or "Green Line"
  West Bank and Gaza Boundary
- "No Man's Land"

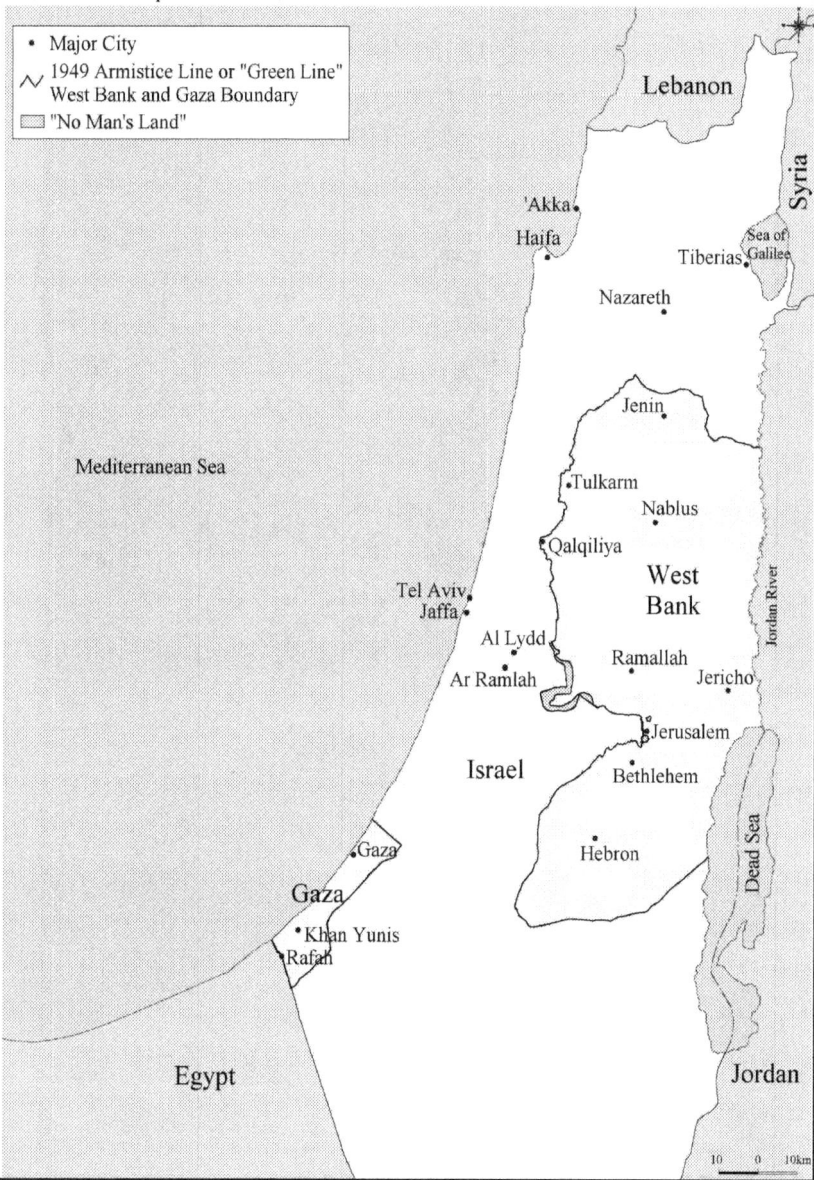

Lebanon

Syria

'Akka

Haifa

Tiberias Sea of Galilee

Nazareth

Jenin

Mediterranean Sea

Tulkarm

Nablus

Qalqiliya

West
Bank

Tel Aviv
Jaffa

Jordan River

Al Lydd

Ramallah

Jericho

Ar Ramlah

Jerusalem

Israel

Bethlehem

Gaza

Hebron

Dead Sea

Gaza

Khan Yunis
Rafah

Egypt

Jordan

10   0   10km

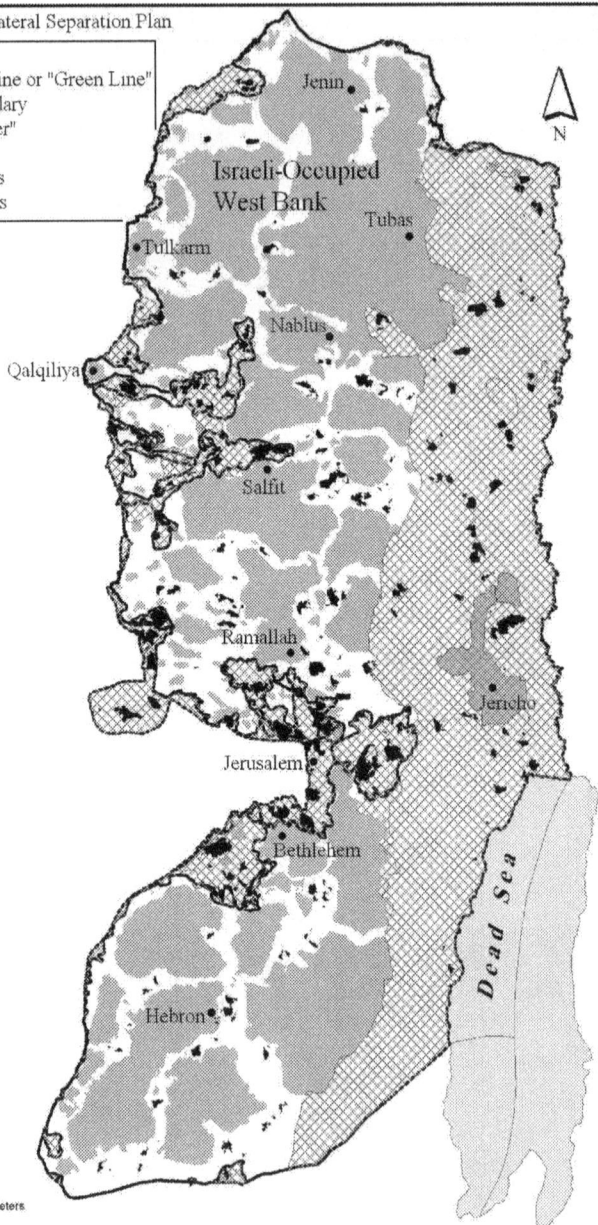

Projection of Israel's Unilateral Separation Plan

- • Major City
- 1949 Armistice Line or "Green Line"
- West Bank Boundary
- "Separation Barrier"
- Palestinian Areas
- Segregation Zones
- Israeli Settlements

N

Jenin

Israeli-Occupied
West Bank

Tubas

Tulkarm

Nablus

Qalqiliya

Salfit

Ramallah

Jericho

Jerusalem

Bethlehem

Dead Sea

Hebron

0   10 Kilometers

The Contributors

Alain Epp Weaver worked with Mennonite Central Committee in the Middle East in various capacities for over eleven years. He lived in the West Bank, Gaza, East Jerusalem, and Amman, Jordan, most recently serving as MCC representative for Palestine, Jordan, and Iraq.

Epp Weaver was born in Boulder, Colorado, and grew up in Lincoln, Nebraska. He graduated from Bethel College (Kansas) in 1991 and received a Master of Divinity from the University of Chicago in 1999. He currently is a doctoral student in theology at the University of Chicago.

Together with his wife Sonia, Epp Weaver wrote *Salt and Sign: Mennonite Central Committee in Palestine, 1949-1999* (Akron, Pa.: MCC, 1999). He edited the volume, *Mennonite Theology in Face of Modernity* and has published articles in academic and popular venues, including *Mennonite Quarterly Review, Journal of Religious Ethics, Review of Politics, Christian Century,* and *The Mennonite.*

Epp Weaver is married to Sonia Weaver. Alain and Sonia have two children, Samuel and Katherine. He is a member of First Mennonite Church of Bluffton, Ohio.

Esther Epp-Tiessen is Peace Ministries Coordinator for MCC Canada. She has served with MCC in the Philippines, Ontario, and Manitoba, and has also worked as a pastor, researcher, and writer. She has a master of arts in Canadian history from the University of Manitoba and has published two books on Canadian Mennonite themes, *Altona: The Story of a Prairie Town* and *J. J. Thiessen: A Leader for his Time.* She is a member of Charleswood Mennonite Church in Winnipeg, Manitoba. She is married to Dan Epp-Tiessen and has two living sons.

Dan Epp-Tiessen is currently assistant professor of Bible at Canadian Mennonite Unversity in Winnipeg, Manitoba. His other work experience includes pastoring, homemaking, and serving as Mennonite Central Committee country representative in the Philippines from 1982-1986 together with his wife Esther.

Timothy Seidel serves as peace development worker with Mennonite Central Committee in the Occupied Palestinian Territories. Seidel was born in California and grew up in Massachusetts. He graduated from Messiah College (Pennsylvania) in 1999 and received a Master of Theological Studies from Wesley Theological Seminary (Washington, D.C.) and a Master of Arts in international peace and conflict resolution from American University's School of International Service (Washington, D.C.) in 2003.

Along with his wife Christi Hoover Seidel, Timothy has lived for the past three years in the West Bank town of Bethlehem, where their son Kai Emanuel was recently born.

Christi Hoover Seidel is currently co-peace development worker for Mennonite Central Committee in the West Bank with her husband Tim. Christi was born and raised in Central Pennsylvania. Her background is in education and behavioral science, and she is a graduate of Messiah College in Pennsylvania. She was a first-grade teacher in Carlisle, Pennsylvania, from 2000-2003. She gave birth to her first child, Kai Emanuel, in Bethlehem, Palestine, in 2006.

www.ingramcontent.com/pod-product-compliance
Lightning Source LLC
Chambersburg PA
CBHW031255090426
42742CB00007B/458